TIGER IN A LION'S DEN

TIGER IN A
LION'S DEN

Adventures in
LSU
Basketball
●

DALE BROWN
with Don Yaeger

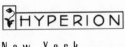
HYPERION
New York

Library of Congress Cataloging-in-Publication Data

Brown, Dale
Tiger in a lion's den : adventures in LSU basketball / Dale Brown with Don Yaeger. — 1st ed.
p. cm.
ISBN 0-7868-6044-8
1. Brown, Dale. 2. Basketball coaches—United States—Biography. 3. Louisiana State University (Baton Rouge, La.)—Basketball—History. I. Yaeger, Don. II. Title.
GV884.B76A3 1994
796.323′092—dc20   94-21629
[B]   CIP

Designed by Claudyne Bianco

First Edition

10 9 8 7 6 5 4 3 2 1

*Thanks to all my players, players'
parents, assistant coaches, associ-
ates, friends, and family for your
trust and help*

DALE BROWN

*To Denise, Billy, and Katie. You
have taught me the connection between home and happiness. I love
you all.*

DON YAEGER

Contents

Contents

Foreword

I have been fortunate to have played basketball for six coaches who are in the Naismith Basketball Hall of Fame. The common thread that links those personalities is that they consider themselves teachers rather than coaches. Interestingly, they rarely speak of or teach basketball. My top coaches always spoke in terms of life's lessons and the values and characteristics that one needs to be successful in their journey. This is the type of coach, teacher, and man that I have personally found Dale Brown to be.

Dale Brown's *Tiger in a Lion's Den* is not a book recapitulating the glorious moments of his lifelong commitment to the world's greatest game, but rather a personal reflection of the difficult moments that confront a proud, educated, determined, and just soul. From limited means to being a struggling school teacher and coach to creating and running one of

Foreword

the nation's most popular and successful college basketball programs, Dale Brown has faced the cruel hatred and jealousy of opponents in life, basketball, business, and death.

Endless battles with mindless bureaucrats at every turn have only strengthened Dale Brown's resolve to do his best when his best was needed most. His impact on people and events is truly an inspiration to us all. His drive for excellence and perfection, his intolerance for mediocrity and failure make us proud to know Dale and learn more of him and from him through this fine book.

Many good things can be said about the man Dale Brown. The best thing that I can do is entrust my eldest son, Adam Walton, to Dale Brown's basketball program at LSU as Adam embarks on his basketball career. I am proud of and happy for both of them. This book gives me even more confidence and reassurance that Adam will find his own success through his own teachers, starting with Dale Brown.

—Bill Walton
June 26, 1994

TIGER IN A
LION'S DEN

Introduction

Samuel Johnson, sometime in the mid-1700s, said, "What is written without effort is in general without pleasure to read." If this is true, my sincere hope is that you will find this book extremely enjoyable to read because I labored long and hard to write each word of each chapter. I have dabbled from time to time with journalism, but only in the sense of a few newspaper columns and an occasional magazine article. The cultivation of each sentence to define each moment so that you see and feel it as I did was a much more challenging task than I had ever envisioned.

My time spent on this project also brought me a great appreciation for those in the print media. Native Americans say "You must walk a mile in another man's moccasins before you can judge him." I found out very quickly the amount of time and energy that must be put forth in writing to secure each and every detail in making sure that all the facts are both true and in sequential order. But now let's throw in a deadline, and here is a new pressure for a coach who thought he knew about all pressures. The journalist who covers his world and must cover it and report it before a deadline each evening is truly a professional and without question those who go the extra mile to report substantiated truth under the deadline are indeed special.

Something else somewhat unexpected also occurred to me as my journey into this project progressed. As I inked down each word or expressed each thought or explained each story, it was if I was taking a strong look into the mirror. The book gave me an opportunity to look at myself at different times in my life and helped me see myself in a different perspective. For many this might seem a bit frightening, but as I often tell my team, staff, family, and friends, quoting Plato, "the unexamined life is not worth living." This process was also extremely therapeutic, a kind of releasing environment where I had an opportunity to say some things that I have often wanted to say but was not given the proper forum. There were events that when looked back upon were extremely difficult. Some rewinds brought a smile of fond remembrance to my face. Other times turned back to brought wide-ranging emotions. But the process was a soul-washing one, and I feel that actually sitting down and writing the book has made me a better man for it; a man who has a different perspective on life and many of my life-shaping events.

Above all, I quickly and sternly came to the revolutionary concept that those events in my life that at the time seemed to be crises were not. This coup was and will be the greatest reward of all for writing this book. There have been so many events that have molded me, yet events that at the time *seemed* nearly life and death, were not. With the passage of time, I came to the realization that they were *only* moments in life that we face, that give us the option to choose a path to follow. The event itself is not nearly as important as how we *handle* the event. From this point on, in light of this discovery, I will view such seemingly difficult times through a different lens.

Finally, it was a goal of mine that this book would cover a lot of bases in regard to its purpose. I wanted to share a behind-the-scenes look at the major college basketball world for the great hoop fans around the country. I wanted to share some inspirational stories that could help motivate those who read the book, whether they love the game of basketball or not. I also wanted to share the other part of the coaching world. And finally, I wanted to share some very treasured moments in my life, especially as the head basketball coach at Louisiana State University.

Above all, I wanted to represent the truth as I saw it. Often, at least in the profession of coaching, many of our actions and feelings go unreported (often because of that *deadline*). This is my opportunity to, as Paul Harvey says, give you "the rest of the story." As it was written in 735 A.D. by Cuthbert's letter to Cuthwin on the death of The Venerable Bede:

> *"There is still one sentence, dear master, that we haven't written down." And he said, "Write it." After a while the boy said, "There, now it is written." "Good,"*
> *he replied. "It is finished, you have spoken the truth."*

This I have tried to do as well. This is my "last sentence."

1

Taking Shots at the Shaq

Ahead by 22 points and with no signs of letting up, I believed that our lead over Tennessee in the quarterfinals of the 1992 SEC (Southeastern Conference) tournament was secure. As a team, we had been playing extremely well, winning 11 of our last 12 games. Now we were dominating Tennessee and Shaquille O'Neal was having his way with Tennessee's smaller center, Carlus Groves.

Tennessee was very talented. Allan Houston was a first-round NBA draft pick, one of the greatest players to ever play in the SEC. Still, I didn't think they could beat us. As the score mounted—our lead was in the mid-20s most of the way—there seemed to be a mounting futility in the way Tennessee was playing.

Suddenly, a game we had under control got out of control. In one of the most bizarre set of circumstances I ever saw in nearly four decades of coaching, everything went wild.

From the sidelines, I watched as our point guard, Jamie Brandon, slipped a perfect bounce pass into Shaquille, who had posted up on Groves. Shaquille took the pass from Jamie, spun to his right and jumped to dunk once again. I couldn't believe my eyes. Groves wrapped his arms around Shaquille's waist and jerked him backwards. I saw Shaq's knee bend awkwardly. I saw his head and shoulders fall backwards. He didn't even get the shot off. My first thought was that this was how Shaquille's career was going to end. I just knew he was going to be injured badly.

I jumped up and the referee blew his whistle; he signaled an intentional foul. I felt that a fight was going to be inevitable. After the call, Groves pulled on Shaquille again, again by his waist. It looked like a takedown move I taught during my days as a high school wrestling coach in North Dakota. I saw Shaquille spin around and sling Groves off his back with his left arm. But I think it is important to say that Shaquille *did not* throw a punch and never did throughout his college career.

The rules state that a coach can go out on the floor to stop a potential fight without getting a technical foul, but the players cannot leave the bench. So I headed out on the floor. As I took my first step onto the court, I looked at Shaquille. I saw a couple of our players along with a referee move him aside. I thought, That's enough. I wanted to go face to face with Groves and let him know what I thought. That was my intention—nothing more. I was hacked.

I made my way over to him and tried to push the referee out of the way to give Groves a piece of my mind. As I did my right hand grazed Groves' left shoulder. I said, "That's the third time you've played this way against us." As I said it, I saw him pull back and prepare to hit me. He drew his left fist back and swung at me. I raised my right arm to stop him. The whole court now exploded. The entire situation was totally out of control. With bodies bumping into each other all over the floor, it looked almost like an old Western barroom brawl. The only thing was, during most all of the fight, no real punches were landed. Everybody was just yapping, pushing, and pulling.

I know I should have controlled my emotions, but in the minds of some in the media, I was automatically wrong. I felt like very few were interested in the truth of the matter, the history of our games against Groves, and my reasons for being so upset. Some of the media accused me of taking a swing at him, which the video clearly proved I had not. And had I done so, I would have been man enough to admit it.

Before the game had even started, I was apprehensive about the situation with Carlus Groves. We had played at Tennessee the prior year and had experienced some trouble with him. When he elbowed Shaquille in the rib cage, Shaquille grabbed his ribs and looked at me. I signaled for him to be calm. I had worked with him on maintaining his composure for months. I continually explained to him that other teams were going to beat up on him, but he must not lose his cool. He kept asking "Coach, why can they beat up on me, but I can't touch them? I am just like a tree. All they do is hang on me." I said, "Shaquille, I understand. And I am going to try and change it."

It was true that all he had to do was simply bump someone and they would call a foul on him. In Arkansas one year, we were tied with just seconds to go in the final game for the SEC West championship. Arkansas had a great team with Todd Day, Oliver Miller, and Lee Mayberry. We had the ball and were going to Shaquille for the last shot, when two guys actually pulled him to the floor, a feat I didn't think Japan's largest sumo wrestler was capable of. It was the only time I had ever seen Shaquille knocked down like that. There was no call. Absolutely no call. It is called swallowing your whistle.

I put together a videotape of Shaquille's greatest hits—I'm talking about intentional fouls, not his platinum rap album—and sent it to the head of SEC officials, John Guthrie. On that tape were several plays involving Carlus Groves.

But what happened in this Tennessee game made all of those other fouls look like child's play. After the screaming and yelling subsided and the players were separated, I realized that all three referees were in a huddle deciding our fate with SEC officials and the television crew. They threw Shaquille and four more of our players out of the game. Of the five, four were starters. Tennessee lost Groves, two starters, and three other role players. Ironically, one of the Tennessee players who was ejected was Alonzo Johnson, who transferred to LSU just last season.

It took at least fifteen minutes to get the game going again. Then Tennessee started rallying on us. I could not believe it. Their player commits an intentional foul, we lose four starters, and now they are climbing back into the game. Our 22-point lead went all the way down to 10 points, with only three minutes to play. Fortunately, we were making our free throws and we ended up winning 99–89. The win sent us into the semifinal game against Kentucky the next day.

I got to the locker room after the game to find out that Shaquille was not only thrown out of that game, but would not be allowed to play against Kentucky in the tournament semifinals. I was stunned. One injustice was enough, and this was too much. Our chancellor, Bud Davis, was there along with our athletic director, Joe Dean. I really wanted to talk to Roy

Kramer, the SEC Commissioner, but he was in the NCAA Basketball Selection Committee meeting in Kansas City. I asked them to get him on the phone.

I had decided that I was not going to take the team out to play the next day against Kentucky unless this injustice was corrected. When we finally got him on the phone I said, "Roy, this is absolutely wrong. This young man has been beaten up all year long. I have told you people in the league that this will eventually cost you one of the great superstars to ever play in our league. He's not going to tolerate this and neither is his family. He will not stay. You have to be fair with the guy, and it's just not fair that he was thrown out of the game against Tennessee and then is thrown out for tomorrow's game against Kentucky too. The perpetrator didn't have a thing to lose. Since Tennessee lost, Groves will not be suspended for a game because their season was over. And now they are asking us to play without Shaquille, who was the *victim*. The system is all screwed up. The rule is wrong. We're just not playing tomorrow, and that's it." Everyone was shocked. The SEC officials saw their tournament going up in smoke; all of their television money and their ticket money. They realized I was serious and I was ready to face any reprimand the league placed on me.

There is no question that the officials have to stop fights, but Shaquille did not start this one and he did not strike anyone. It was an unfortunate incident and in my opinion there were several reasons for such a severe penalty. One was that Shaquille dominated everyone and got no sympathy from the referees, a second was that I have been considered a maverick in this league.

I don't want to be a martyr, a cry baby, or transfer blame but I felt deeply about this situation. The intentional foul rule gives players a license to get away with brutal fouls and the retaliation rule is unfair to a player who responds in self-defense.

Executive Associate Commissioner Mark Womack was sympathetic as he tried to calm me down. "I am not calming down!" I exclaimed. I looked him right in the eye and told him we were not going out to play the next day. John Guthrie pulled me aside and tried his logic. I said, "John, there was an injustice committed out there and I have been telling you all year that Shaquille was being manhandled." I told John I was going to the postgame press conference to make my announcement and to advise Shaquille to get out of this league before he got seriously injured.

I took off for the press conference. On the way out the door, my daughter, Robyn, said, "Daddy, don't say anything at the press conference about not playing. Think about it before you make your final decision." I told her that my decision was made.

As I walked into the press conference, though, I realized she was right. If I announced we weren't playing, I couldn't reverse the decision. So I decided to be silent. Still, I was really mad. The atmosphere in the press room was hostile. No one asked me about Carlus Groves, they only asked me about my and Shaquille's reactions. I couldn't bite my tongue any longer. I said that enough was enough, and that after this ridiculous incident it was time for Shaquille O'Neal to move on to the NBA before his career was ended by a flagrant foul. I would recommend to his family that the Tennessee game be his last in the SEC. Well, some of the writers just went nuts.

I went back to my hotel room and Joe Dean asked me what I was going to do. I still stood firmly by my decision not to play. Bud Davis and Joe Dean said they wanted me to think about it because they believed I was making a mistake. They just asked me to use good judgment. Robyn was again my voice of reason. She said, "Daddy, not showing up is exactly what some people will want you to do. Kentucky wants to win that tournament without having to play against you." I thought about it and said, "You are right, Robyn. We are going to play." I called Joe Dean and said, "I'm going to go ahead and play." I could tell Joe was relieved, and I thanked him for his support.

When I walked out on that court the next day, I felt like a Christian being thrown to the lions. The crowd started to boo. "Throw Dale out," they were yelling. "Throw Dale out." All it did was fire me up. If I were to single out the worst experience in my coaching career, it would be that day when my daughter had to sit in the stands and hear them calling for her father to be thrown out. It was unquestionably the meanest and most difficult on-court incident in my career. To make it all worse, they wouldn't even allow Shaquille to sit on the bench. I thought that was also absolutely ludicrous.

Despite it all, we had Kentucky on the ropes, even without Shaquille. The game went to the wire and we lost by six points, 80–74. Rick Pitino was most complimentary after the game regarding our team's inspired play. The whole matter, though, took the air right out of the sails of a team that was playing extremely well. I thought we were coming together well and were going to go far in the NCAA tournament. But though we beat BYU in the first round, we lost to Indiana in the second.

In retrospect, my temper took me onto the court to a certain extent, but my ethics took me out there more than my temper. I thought what happened was wrong. I thought Carlus Groves was trying to take Shaquille out of the game for good by hurting him. So they lose Carlus Groves and we lose Shaquille O'Neal. That's like their losing a thimble and our losing the Hope Diamond. That doesn't make any sense.

Then the articles came out. I was hammered, but some

12

●

neat things came up, too. One great story came from Roy Exum, the executive sports editor of the Chattanooga *News-Free Press* and one of the classiest men I've met in this business. He told me that after the Tennessee game, he went to a function and sent his thirteen-year-old son off to eat with several sports writers that were his friends. His table was Dale Brown–bashing, and all of a sudden his little son said to these sports writers, "I don't care what any of you say, that's the kind of coach I want to play for. He's someone that would always defend you." They all were quiet.

I was walking through the airport a couple of weeks after the incident and I stopped to watch an NCAA playoff game on television. A porter was standing close by and I felt him staring at me. Pretty soon he asks if I'm the basketball coach at LSU. He then whistles and called about three of his friends over. "Oh man," he said, "my friends and I watched that game against Tennessee. We loved it. What you did was great. I wish I had a son. I'd send him to you." That was another positive.

Many mothers have told me that one of the reasons that they were interested in their sons attending LSU was because they knew I would stand up for them.

Hindsight is 20/20. But in retrospect, I wished I hadn't done it. I didn't mean to cause that much pain to my family or cripple our team in any way, and I also did not want to hurt Carlus Groves. I wrote to Carlus, who transferred to San Diego State, and to his parents telling them I was sorry for what happened. I never heard anything from them. I also called Wade Houston, the Tennessee coach, to apologize. He was very understanding. I sincerely wish I would have handled the whole incident more tactfully. I'm not very suave, and I don't look for the smooth routes anywhere in life.

It wasn't the first time I've taken up for someone in my basketball family. Nor, likely, will it be the last. Once, when I was still in college, we were playing against a real good player named Luther Aamold. We had a player on our team, a really good basketball player, named Henry Milkey. He could have played big time. I was on the bench with foul trouble, a position I often found myself in. Luther and Henry had quite a battle going and late in the game, Luther knocked Henry to the floor. I reacted instantly, jumping off the bench and charging at Luther. I pulled Luther by his jersey one way and back the other. To make a long story short, I got a technical foul and the coach bawled me out. But Aamold's jersey was stretched up and down and he looked like Madonna wearing one of her outfits with the low-cut tops. You could not even see his number. Aamold left Milkey alone the rest of the game.

I guess both the Carlus Groves and Luther Aamold incidents are reflective of two traits that are, at least in my opinion, my greatest strength and my greatest weakness. My strength is my loyalty to those who are part of my family. Too many people today aren't committed to their friends. I am not a warm-weather friend. I'm committed to those I love—all the way. Some people pointed out how silly it was for me to run out and try and defend Shaquille, one of the biggest and strongest men in basketball. The fact that Shaq could fend for himself didn't matter one bit. I love him and I'll fight for him any day of the week when he is in the right.

My weakness is my quick temper. I am not going to hesitate to make a decision. I am going to make a decision and I would just as soon be wrong than late. I can handle being wrong. But most people are late because they are calculating how they can look their best in every situation. They think of how they can sound good to the media. I'm the opposite, and to a certain extent, I'm sorry that I am.

When you grow up having to fight for everything, it's hard to put your fists down and use your brain. I overreact more than most people because I saw pain as a young kid and could do nothing about it. It was frustrating. I've always had a very short fuse when it comes to injustice of any kind. But there is a better way of dealing with situations. I just have to learn how to do it. Most often, I get aggressive and candid like a typical North Dakotan. Roger Maris, who grew up in Fargo, North Dakota, once told me that it took him until the twilight of his career to learn this same lesson.

I have to admit I've learned some important lessons through all this. I should show more patience. Most of the things I do, I do from my heart, but that doesn't necessarily mean my actions are correct. I do represent the team, and I don't want our players to act like me when I'm wrong. It's very important to keep my emotions under control if I am leading people. If I'm teaching the players not to display their emotions, then I can't be a hypocrite.

The noted educator William Lyon Phelps probably said it best: "Teaching is an art so great and so difficult to master that a man can spend a lifetime at it, without realizing much more than his limitations and mistakes, and his distance from the ideal."

I'm still learning.

2

Why Not Minot

If ever one human being could be without sin, I grew up with her. My mother, Agnes Brown, was the single most pathologically honest person I ever met; the most kind person who has ever lived. I remember watching her return 40 cents and a quarter to the grocery store when she had been given too much change. She never spoke unkindly about another human being, she never talked about her husband who left her, she wasn't bitter, she never smoked, she never drank, and she never had a date. She had a terrible inferiority complex and allowed most people to beat her down. I thought that was a weakness in her. I wanted her to stand up for herself; I wanted it for her in the worst way. But she just wasn't an assertive person. I've never understood how I could be so different. While I loved my mother, I've always despised weakness.

The older I get, the more I realize that my mother was a

tremendous influence on me. As a result, the one thing that I always tell our players is to appreciate their mothers fully. I did not understand then what a struggle my mother had, and what a fabulous woman she was. I wish now that I would have appreciated her more.

Her inferiority complex, I believe, is directly responsible for my protective nature. Never do I want to cower, as she did, from injustice. Nor will I let those I love fear injustice. That defensiveness surfaced one day when I was eight years old. I was required to come home from school for lunch every day. One day when I got home, Mother was rocking in her chair and wringing her hands, as she did when she was worried. She said, "Dale, you have to be very careful. The landlady is going to kick me out of the apartment." "What for, Mama?" I asked. Since there were no basketball goals in our neighborhood, I used to take mittens and socks and fold them up to use as basketballs. There were hot water pipes in the hallway of the apartment building, and I would shoot the mittens over the pipes, using the pipes as a basket. The floors in the hallway were linoleum, and I'd scuff them with my shoes as I was play-ing basketball. My mother continued, "The landlady said that you can't be out there playing anymore because you scuff the linoleum in the hallway. She is going to kick us out of here, Dale, and we don't have any other place to live." I strode down to apartment number four and knocked on the landlady's door. She had a little peephole that she opened up and said "Yes." I said, "I want to talk to you." She opened the door. I started in, "Don't you ever, ever talk to my mother like that again. You hear me?" Then I turned and walked slowly down the hallway, dragging my heels the whole way and scuffing that precious linoleum.

What really set me off, however, was that welfare worker that used to come and see Mom. She always wore a black dress, and she was very rude and dominating. I was a small boy sitting in the kitchen eating a bowl of soup when I overheard her giving my mother hell about the amount of money the state was giving us for welfare. She even made Mother open her purse to see if she was hiding any money. My mother was sitting in her rocker with her head hung low. She was scared; she had no money, and no education. She worked a few days a week cleaning homes and babysitting, and received no support from her husband. Mom had a hard time seeing the blue sky and the green grass because she was so concerned about where the next nickel was coming from. The welfare lady sneered, "I want to say something else to you. Do you realize that last month you spent thirteen dollars on digitalis?" I learned that word as a young kid. It was her heart medicine. The lady continued, "How do you expect Ward County Welfare to continue paying that? After all, you get forty-two-fifty a month from welfare." I was watching her the whole time, and the more I saw my mother cry, the more I thought, "What gives you the right to treat another human being like that?" Then the welfare lady glanced over at me and said "Can't he work?" My mother started to cry harder and she told the lady that I did work, selling papers. I made a promise to myself sitting right there, that for the rest of my life I would never let anyone intimidate me or do wrong to any of my friends. I wanted so badly to just run over and kick that woman. I felt sorry for my mother and wished I was bigger and could do more. I thought that if that's how the damn system works, then I was going to whip the system.

My mother and I lived in a one-room apartment in downtown Minot. Not a one-bedroom apartment, just a one-room apartment with a tiny kitchen about the size of a refrigerator box. You had to go down the hall and share the toilet and bath with a dozen other people. My two older sisters lived nearby.

But we were warm and secure, and we were together. Later, when I was a teenager, we moved to a larger apartment and had our own bath and toilet, which I thought was the height of luxury.

From the moment the doctor snipped the umbilical cord, my mother wanted me to be an altar boy. I can still repeat every altar boy prayer today. But I had a problem with the way the church used to recognize those who put money in the offering. My church used to have a gold page, a green page and a yellow page in the bulletin. The gold page was for those who gave the most, the green for the second most, and so on. They would spell out on those pages how much you had given. Well, my mother didn't have anything, but she'd always dig out a few cents to put in her envelope. At the end of the year my mom was always near the bottom of the list. She may only have given a few dollars all year long, and it embarrassed her that she was unable to give more.

I developed my own little program for earning pocket money. I would stand in front of the bar below our apartment complex with a lasso and a water gun. I would throw the lasso at the men going in the bar with their dates and I would say, "Okay, before you go on you have got to give me a dime." Their girlfriends would always say, "Oh, isn't he cute," and I'd get my dime. It's called survival.

When you have to survive, any job looks good and I've had my share of them, such as:

- gandy dancer on the railroad, tamping ties and straightening rails
- janitor in a jewelry store
- hide and fur company—common laborer
- shoeshine boy in the basement of a hotel
- laborer at a foundry that made culverts

19

- hotel bellman
- carryout boy in a grocery store
- paper boy on street corners
- creamery, checking in trucks before and after their routes
- building grain elevators
- cab driver
- cleaned cisterns that held water for homes
- washed athletic equipment for Minot State Teachers College (now the University)
- batboy for a semipro baseball team
- drove a school bus (even though I didn't have a driver's license at the time and didn't know how to use a stick shift)
- cleaned out barns and baled hay
- maintenance work for a city park
- drove a cement truck
- tarred roofs
- truckdriver and delivery man for a bottling company
- referee for recreation department (Can you believe this one?)
- delivery boy in furniture auction store
- delivered flyers for department stores

Using the socks to play basketball worked well until I was in fifth grade. That's when I got my first real basketball through a Sears, Roebuck contest. It was one of the old kinds with a lace. That really got me started; I was hooked. Then I got on my first recreation league team and we won the city championship, beating my future Minot State teammate, Henry Milkey, and his team in the final game. We won 14–12, and I shot two crucial free throws on my knees. I think they were the two free throws that won the game.

Why Not Minot

I learned from my mother the importance of being honest. Sometimes I think I learned it too well. Once, as junior at Minot State Teachers College, we were driving back from a game and we decided to grab a six-pack of beer. We used to carpool with six in a car, but this was the first trip that I wasn't riding in the coach's car or the radio announcer's car. We stopped at a little store and everybody in the car had a beer. We threw the cans away before we got back to the hotel. Coach Herb Parker was waiting for us when we finally got back. He called me over and asked, "Where have you guys been?" Then he asked point-blank, "Have you been drinking?" I looked at him and said "Yes." Immediately, he told me I wouldn't be playing the rest of the season. Everyone else who was in the car started flipping out. They thought I was going to turn them in. I could have lied and it might have been fine; nothing would have happened. But that wasn't the way I was taught to act.

After Herb suspended me from the team, I made up my mind I was going to do one of two things. I was either going to transfer to the University of North Dakota, or enlist in the Marines. So I went to the recreation department to talk to my friend and mentor, Reuben Hammond, who was the director. I was embarrassed and mad at the same time. But my decision was firm, I was going to leave. I'll never forget what he did. He put his arm around me, and said, "Let me just say something to you. I never believed in kicking a guy in the head when he is down, but don't you ever walk away from trouble. Face the situation, hold your head up, and keep on." It was just like somebody had pumped adrenaline into my veins. I said, "You are right. Why am I feeling sorry for myself? I did the right thing by admitting the truth. I can't blame anyone." That moment with him gave me a future.

My wife and daughter think I've probably said too much

on the subject of growing up without a father. But the fact that my father left my mother two days before she gave birth to me obviously played an important role in developing some of my opinions about family and loyalty. I saw my father as someone who lacked loyalty. As a result, I am loyal myself and respect loyalty in others. In fact, sometimes my loyalty is blind, almost to a fault.

When I was ten years old, I experienced my first feelings about my father. My mother was out babysitting one night and I was snooping through her papers. She had a Bible in one of her drawers and in it was a letter. I didn't read the letter because it was in an envelope. In the upper left hand corner was the name Charles A. Brown, 302 East Ash, Enid, Oklahoma. I wondered who that was. I thought it might be my father, but since I had never asked my mother his name, I wasn't sure. It was almost as if he were dead. I had learned to spell the word *deceased* at a very early age, because that was what I wrote on everything that asked for my father's name; I was embarrassed that I didn't have a father in the house.

When she came home from babysitting I asked her, "Who's Charles A. Brown?" I distinctly remember her slowly putting down her purse and saying, "Why do you ask?" I said, "I was just wondering." She said, "That's your father." I left the room and crawled out on the fire escape. I had a twinge of pain, but it passed quickly; I was determined that I wouldn't let him hurt me like he had hurt her. After that incident, I was never curious about him again. I really didn't care about him, except every year during the father-son banquet at school. The kids without fathers were taken to the banquet by some thoughtful men in the community. It was embarrassing. I hated it. It was demeaning. There were all those kids with their real fathers. It also bothered me at the beginning of hunting season each year because the guys would go hunting with their fathers. I couldn't go hunting, so I just buried the painful feelings.

Eventually I came to dislike my father, even though I had never met him. Then one day when I was a senior in high school, there was a knock on the door of my Latin class. Up to that time, I had never talked to my father. I had never seen a picture of him. I had never gotten a letter from him. The priest answered the door. I was in the last row of desks in the classroom. I heard somebody say "Is Dale Brown here?" I thought "Oh no, what did I do now?" I slumped in my desk. Father came in and said, "Dale, there is someone here to see you." I walked out in the hall and there was this man; he was bigger than me and was well dressed and handsome. He said, "Are you Dale Brown?"

I had no idea who he was. I looked him in the eye and answered, "Yes." He stuck his hand out to shake and said, "I'm your father." I will never forget the emotion. I wanted to punch him. I wanted to cry. I was embarrassed. But I responded by being a smart ass. "Is that right, well I'm my own grandpa." That was a popular phrase we used then. Then I turned around and walked away. My reaction was a complete coverup.

I made my way back into the classroom, but I was shell-shocked. At noon, I went home for lunch and there he was, sitting with my mother. She had my soup on the table—she had it timed perfectly—she knew exactly how many minutes it took me to get home for lunch. So I started to eat my soup, but I looked at him the whole time. I distinctly remember him telling her, "Well, Agnes, he's a fine-looking boy. You can be proud of him. You know I'm going to make it up to you, Agnes. I have some land and I have some money now, and I'm going to give it to you." I just sat there and watched. She was very attentive, very nice. I finished my soup, got up, told my mother goodbye and I left. I didn't see him again for eight years.

In 1961, I was called into the army for the Berlin Crisis and sent to Ft. Riley, Kansas. Soon after, I had a three-day pass. Lying around in the barracks on a Saturday, I suddenly blurted out, "302 East Ash, Enid, Oklahoma."

I asked an army buddy if he'd do me a favor and go with me to Enid, Oklahoma. "What the hell do I want to go to Enid, Oklahoma, for?" he asked. I said, "Well, the man that brought me on this earth lives there." Now I had not called, and I had not written. I had seen his address as a ten-year-old in my mother's Bible.

When we arrived in Enid, Oklahoma, we stopped by a drugstore that had a pay phone booth. I went in, opened up the directory, and there it was, Charles A. Brown, 302 East Ash, and the number. I put the money in and dialed the number. A woman answered the phone. I asked if Charles Brown was there. "Just a minute," she said. Shortly, a man answered the phone. I said, "Is this Mr. Brown?" "Yes it is," he answered. "Who's this?" I replied, "This is Dale Brown from Minot, North Dakota." "Oh, Dale! Where are you?" he asked. "I'm in Enid, Oklahoma, I want to come by and see you." He gave me directions to his house.

When we drove up, he was standing on his porch by the screen door waiting for us. We got out of the car and he started walking down the steps. "Which one is my son?" he asked. I said, "I'm Dale," and I shook his hand. He invited us in to meet his wife and she was very nice. We were just chit-chatting and small talking, when I decided to get off my chest what I had been carrying around for years.

I said, "Mr. Brown, can I talk to you for a minute?" We went out into the yard and I said, "I just want to tell you why I came. I'm curious to see how you could abandon a baby two daughters and a wife, and I'm curious to see if you had any curiosity about what I was doing in life. I mean, did you ever want to see what I looked like? Did you want a picture? Did you want to see me play ball? And I also came here to tell you something." He said, "Well Dale, I did wrong by your mother. She is a beautiful woman. I had such a guilt complex. I just could not face your mother. I could not face you. I know it was a mistake and I apologize." I said, "There was a time when I could have whipped you for how you treated us. But now I'm over that and I just want you to know you can die knowing this: I totally forgive you. I will make certain that I never lack loyalty to friends or family, no matter what. You have cemented the fact that I'll keep my marriage and my family together, no matter what hardships or difficulties occur."

Well he was very nice, and he thanked me. I drove off and that was the end of it. That was the last time I ever saw him. He died a few years later. It was really strange—when he died I was unemotional. I had no hatred, no love, no sadness, no happiness, no bitterness. I still include him in my prayers.

But for all that, I recognize now that I had it made as a little boy. There was no child abuse and never any anger in my home. My mother never raised her voice. I didn't see fighting. I recognize that my childhood wasn't as tough as I thought it was compared to so many others. Most importantly, I was taught values from a mother who had values that were untouchable.

But despite the lack of interest from my own father, the truth is that I was blessed with several people who cared for and about me. The three men who had the greatest impact on my early life were Monsignor John Hogan, Reuben Hammond and Herb Parker. In addition to being superintendent at my school, Monsignor Hogan also taught the religion class at eight every morning. One morning, Father was teaching about morality. During this particular religion class he was talking about what impure thoughts are. He was talking about lust, and he said that sex should only occur during marriage. Then in my nine o'clock class I caught myself looking down the blouse of this girl, trying to see her breasts. I felt like a pervert. It was on my conscience all day.

As soon as school was over I ran to Father Hogan's house. I said, "Father, I must be a bad person." "What's wrong," he asked. I said, "You had religion class today on impure thoughts and then I went to my very next class and I tried to look down this girl's blouse." "How old are you?" he asked. I thought, "He's going to tell me I'm going to hell." I told him I was twelve. "Get out of here and come back with something important," he said. "I was doing that at ten." He slapped me in the back of my head and told me to go home. I told myself that that's the way I wanted to be—I'm going to be honest with people, but respect their human nature. My admiration for him grew immensely.

I learned several things from that experience. I learned that while we all need to be disciplined, we're all going to make mistakes. He could have condemned me, but instead he recognized I'd learn a better lesson if he let me know I was human. He didn't make me feel dirty.

Monsignor Hogan seemed to make it his job to try and teach me lessons. When I was a junior in high school, I was the class president and had to lead the junior-senior prom. Some of my buddies were riding me mercilessly about who I was going to take as my date. "I'm not taking any of these pigs to the prom, so I'm not going." The truth is I didn't know how to dance, I had to have a friend of mine teach me how. Two, I didn't have a suit. On the day of the dance, my mother went out and bought me a suit at a rummage sale. It flagrantly smelled of moth balls. In fact, it smelled so badly that everybody thought there was a gas leak in the building.

Why Not Minot

It somehow got back to Monsignor Hogan that I'd said the girls were pigs, so one day in class he told all the girls to turn around and look at me. Then he instructed me to stand up. I stood up and he asked me, "What did you say about going to the junior-senior prom? What did you say about the girls in your class?" He made me say it in front of them, that I had called them pigs. Then he said, "Well, if Dale Brown ever wins another elected position in this school, all you girls must be stupid." Needless to say, I didn't win any elections from that day on. That's why I loved him. He was straight up and hard hitting, right to the point. But boy, when you were right, he'd defend you and if you were wrong he'd tell you. I learned to respect that. Can you imagine what would happen if everyone had to publicly answer for the things they said behind someone's back? Whew!

One thing no one seemed able to stop me from doing, though, was speaking my mind, no matter the circumstances. One time, during a seventh grade recreation league basketball game, there was a referee that I thought was making some bad calls. He didn't want to run up and down the court. One time down the court the ball went out of bounds. He was all the way down at the other end. He slowly walked to get it, and I said, "Mister, he dribbled that ball out. That should be our ball." He made a real smart gesture with his hands instead of admitting that he might have missed it. So the next time he missed a call, I responded with, "Well, you're a lazy son of a bitch." Then I ran down the court. The referee just turned and left the game, and went straight to Reuben Hammond's office to tell on me. Reuben came out and called me to the sideline. He asked me if I had called the referee a son of a bitch. "Yep," I said. Just that.

Reuben said, "Dale, I don't know how much longer you should play. You know you must show respect for the officials. When someone is in charge, they're in charge." Reuben threw me out of the gym so I went across the street to Alm's Dairy Shop. When I came back, Reuben and the referee were standing next to Father E.J. Becwar. He was the principal of my school, St. Leo's. Father Becwar was a big man. He said, "Dale, did you call the referee a son of a bitch?" Again, I just said, "Yep." Boom, he slapped me right across the mouth. I was eating my ice cream and when he hit me the cone started coming out of my mouth. I remember Reuben yelling, "Oh Father!" because he thought Father had knocked my teeth out. Father Becwar simply said, "Dale Brown will shape up," and he walked away.

I remember thinking that I deserved the slap. Most kids would have denied saying it. I could have lied about it, but I told the truth and I suffered the consequences. I guess I should have known I was destined to have referee problems from that point on.

At St. Leo's as a senior, I was first team all-state and a member of the 1953 Catholic All-American high school team in basketball. I led the state in scoring, breaking the North Dakota basketball scoring record. I averaged 21 points a game, and when the Fargo *Forum* and the Minot paper came out and printed stories under headlines BROWN CLINCHES CLASS A SCORING CHAMPIONSHIP I felt important for the first time. I knew then that athletics gave me a sense of worth.

Several colleges talked to me about a scholarship, but it really wasn't a very tough choice deciding where I would go. Dr. Erenfeld in town had some connections at Marquette and Tulane and he told me I could get scholarships to those schools with his assistance. Well, I knew I wasn't going to either of those places. I couldn't go five feet from home. I didn't have any money or proper clothes. The coach from the University of North Dakota recruited me. Their campus is in Grand Forks, about two hundred miles from Minot. They wanted me to play two sports, football and basketball. I went to the University on my recruiting visit and I never felt so inferior in my life. They had us stay at a fraternity house. It seemed like everyone had a car. They all had money in their pockets. I'll never forget the night we were sitting at the fraternity house eating dinner. We were going to some event afterward. This guy came in and said "Whose sports car is blocking me in?" It was one of those models that I had only heard of, never seen. The guy eating next to me yelled out that it belonged to him, and just go ahead and move it. I watched him drive out with this beautiful car. I was totally intimidated. I couldn't wait to get home and go to Minot State Teachers College, a small school of only five hundred students.

Obviously, the first and most important thing to me when I went to college was athletics. I earned twelve letters in four years, one each year in basketball, football and track, becoming the first and last athlete at Minot to do that in those three sports. My real athletic love, not suprisingly, was basketball. While I started at forward for four years, I wasn't a real star. I didn't have much of a shot, especially compared to some of the other good players on the team. But I had good fundamentals. I knew how to block out and play good defense. I loved to rebound and could hit the open man. My greatest contribution, however, was my desire to win. Coach Parker was one of the best coaches I've ever been around. He taught us the game. During my four years, we won 71 of 95 games. One year we went to the NAIA national tournament.

In addition to athletics, I became serious about academics for the first time. I was a sophomore and I had enrolled in a U.S. History class with Dr. Nels Lillehaugen. I had never been stimulated academically, not one ounce. In class, Dr. Lillehaugen made history exciting and vibrant. He was so good that I told him one day after class that his course had gotten me more interested in school than I ever had been before. I even tried to change my major to history at the end of my sophomore year. I know now, however, what it was that made him so good: he showed an interest in me. He once wrote on a test paper, "Dale, you're a very talented young man. See me after class." I went to him after class and he said, "I can tell you've got a good mind by the way you answered these essay questions." He was the first person to give me a shock treatment on how interesting learning can be and to build my confidence up.

His teaching style was a lot like Dr. T. Harry Williams, a history professor at LSU who won a Pulitzer Prize in 1970 for his book on Huey Long. I sat in on Harry's class one night. As soon as the bell rang, Harry started in. "Lincoln went over to the windows in the White House, it was snowing outside. He was a big man, probably could have played basketball, large hands; he walked to the corner of his desk, put his hand on his chin." He went on for the entire class like that. Everyone, myself included, was hanging on his every word. I sat there listening to him and thought that it was exactly what teaching should be like. He had charisma and an ability to make everything interesting. I remember sitting there when the class was over, and not believing it had gone on for two hours.

In 1954, I became serious, too, about Vonnie Ness, the most beautiful girl I had ever seen. I was a sophomore and she was a freshman when I first saw her. She was registering for the Lutheran Students' Association. I walked up the steps trying to be smooth, which I wasn't. I had my letterman's jacket on, and I looked at her sideways, trying not to be too obvious. She had her hair back in a cute look and had a great figure. Then she just walked off. I asked to see the signup sheet, and I copied Vonnie's name and her telephone number down. I waited about a week and I called her. I figured she'd be impressed by a call from the big man on campus. Well, she wasn't at all impressed. She didn't really give me the time of day. I said, "Would you like to go to a movie sometime?" "Oh, I don't know, I don't even know who you are," she said. I was crushed, but I just acted like it was no big deal. The more I thought about her, the more I became interested in her. Finally, she agreed to go out with me. It wasn't long before we were dating pretty seriously. Sometimes it seemed I tried to screw everything up. I'd miss dates and wouldn't ask her to go on dates and showed up late and dated other people. She finally just told me to get lost, but she was very nice about it. Everyone was infatuated with Vonnie. She was runner-up for Miss North Dakota, she won the talent contest, she won the congeniality award, she was a cheerleader, an honor student, from a small town on the Montana-Canadian border.

When she told me to take a hike, it was the first time it dawned on me that I really was in love with her. But I didn't want to ever say I was in love, because I hadn't even told my mother I loved her. *Love* was a really hard word for me to say. Vonnie was packing groceries and running the register at a grocery store right down the street from the college. I went down there one night and bought a pack of gum. As I walked through the checkout line I said, "Hi. Can I walk you home after work?" She said sure. So I walked her home and I told her I was really sorry and that I was wrong. That was the first time I ever said I was sorry. Then I told her I loved her. It was the first time I ever told anybody on earth that I loved them. We made up and it was the best thing that ever happened to me.

Vonnie really helped settle me down. When you love someone, you have a tendency to become more compassionate and more sensitive, and more calm. Vonnie was always very candid and honest with me, and I think it gave me a certain peace. Vonnie fell in love with me when I had no worldly possessions.

When Vonnie started dating me, she was being rushed by a sorority. I didn't know until years later that the dean of women at Minot State warned Vonnie not to date me. Vonnie told me just a few years ago about the story. She said when she was a freshman, the dean of women called her in the office and said, "Vonnie, you're not gonna get into a sorority. You're running around with this Dale Brown. You know, he had a bad reputation, his mother's on welfare, they don't have anything and he's kind of a wild guy."

The reason Vonnie finally told me this story was because I had received a call from Minot State asking me to be the honored guest at a banquet, and accept the college's Golden Deeds Award for outstanding alumni. I talked for quite a long time with the university president before agreeing to come, and after I hung up Vonnie asked who I had been talking with. When I told her, I wondered out loud whether that dean of women was going to be there. Then she told me about the story. I was actually very hurt.

I invited my two sisters, their husbands, a few other friends, and Dee Dee Govan to sit at the head table. When I was at Minot State, Dee Dee ran a little restaurant. The back of the restaurant was used for prostitutes. Sometimes I'd take Vonnie down to the restaurant when I had no money, and I'd order. Then I'd jingle a couple of coins in my pocket so it looked to Vonnie like I was paying, but Dee Dee would give me the food for free. In Minot, it was interesting that while some men would come by to do business in the back of the restaurant with Dee Dee, they would never acknowledge him on the street. I liked Dee Dee, but I didn't like the way people treated him. So into this banquet walks Dee Dee with white hair, wearing a canary-colored suit with long gold glasses hanging on a long gold chain, and a vest. He's a nice looking man. Everyone was shocked that he was my guest.

The university president got up to introduce me, and you would have thought he introduced Mother Teresa and Saint Francis of Assisi all rolled into one. When he finally sat down I said, "President Olson, I really want to thank you. That's a wonderful tribute." And I continued, "Gee, that greeting doesn't seem fitting for a kid whose own wife was warned by one of our own faculty not to date him a few years back. My wife told me a little story before I arrived that I'd like to share with you." I went on to tell the story about the dean of women. I didn't use any names though. I don't know if she was even there, but it felt good to get it off my chest.

At the end of the banquet, I saw hypocrisy reign again. There was a reception line, and the guests had to file past the guest of honor and those at his table. There was Dee Dee Govan standing in the reception line. He would look at some of the men, address them by their first name and ask how they were doing. When he did, the wives started looking at their husbands like someone was going to have to answer some questions later.

To this day, I try to get home to North Dakota at least once a year. It is virtually a cleansing experience. The people there are brutally honest and hard working. Thomas Wolfe was wrong when he wrote *You Can't Go Home Again*. I believe it depends on how you pack for the trip. If you pack all the bad memories, then you can't go home. But I've got great memories about those days and I'll always return to my birthplace.

3

From the Bottom of the Ladder

Growing up, I never saw myself as a coach. All I ever dreamed of from the time I was a young boy was being an FBI agent. I had great visions of going out and arresting every top criminal. I thought it was exciting. I saw all the FBI movies. But then I was told you needed a law degree to get a job with the FBI, and Minot State was a teachers college. About the only thing you could do with a degree from Minot was teach. So I wound up going into education. When it hit me that I would become a teacher, I really put my mind into becoming a coach. I had been coaching the junior varsity team at St. Leo's since I was seventeen, so I already loved the job. Besides, what better teaching job could there be?

After graduating from Minot, superintendents came from all over the state to interview graduates for teaching and coaching positions. The superintendent from Columbus High

School, Lynn Triplett, was one who offered me a job. He told me he had an opportunity as the head basketball coach, head track coach, and high school principal for $4,700 a year. I thought $4,700 was all the money in the world. I had never owned a car, had never lived anywhere except with my mother. So this just seemed like heaven. I took the job and I bought a 1951 two-door Ford coupe for $300. I had it painted baby blue. Boy, I thought that was the niftiest thing in the world. I was still a year away from marrying Vonnie. I packed that car and I headed for Columbus, North Dakota.

I drove into Columbus with more butterflies than you can ever imagine. It was the same town my wife was from. Her parents still lived there. I couldn't believe I finally had a chance to make some money, and that I had a team. I just kept thinking, "I got a job, a full-time job doing something I love." I rented a flat in a home near the school. I had my own bed for the first time in my life. I taught history, science, and physical education. Since there was no football, I started a wrestling program and almost won the state title. We won the basketball conference championship and ended the season 24–2. I thought we could have won the state championship. We lost to a team in the playoffs, Powers Lake, that we beat three times during the year.

I look back now and I see that no one could start any further down the coaching ladder than I did. But what I love about having started there is it shows you can start from rock bottom and go to the top without kissing anybody's behind or selling your soul. I'm proud that they even gave me that job. America is still the land of opportunity.

During the summers I needed to work on my master's degree, so I drove to Oregon. Since there was no such thing as a coaching school, I wanted to go to the toughest physical education school available. The two toughest physical education schools were the University of Iowa and the University of Oregon. I drove out to Oregon for school every summer to get my master's degree.

After two years at Columbus, Father Blaine Cook came north and offered me a job at my high school alma mater, Bishop Ryan (St. Leo's). The job was to be head basketball coach and assistant football and assistant track coach. The head football coach at Ryan was Ron Erhardt, who went on to become head coach at North Dakota State University, and then the New England Patriots. I earned $5,000 and went home to Minot, which was something I had dreamed of.

What a small world it is. While I was coaching at Bishop Ryan, we played Williston High School. Williston's star player was Phil Jackson, who went on to play for the Knicks and now coaches the Chicago Bulls. He was six feet nine and no one could stop him. As I tried to come up with a game plan, I developed a defense that I named the Freak Defense. He was just so big and so good, I knew we had to do something to neutralize him. So I ran off on our ditto machine diagram after diagram after diagram of a basketball court. I sat with those courts and I fooled around, and I fooled around, and fooled around, and finally I decided that I should use changing defenses. But I wanted to do more than that. I should confuse them on how you change defenses. I came up with the idea of determining which defense we would play based upon which side of the court the ball went to first. In other words, if the ball went into the right side, we'd use a man to man, if it went into the middle we'd use a 1-3-1, and if it went to the left we would play a 2-3 trap. Then during every time out I would use what I called a single clue flip flop. Now if the opponent started to figure out our strategy, I would then change the defenses. I would move the 1-3-1 to the right, move the 2-3 trap to the middle and the man to man to the left. It confused the heck out of people. It neutralized many talented opponents. It started out innocently, just trying to defend Phil Jackson. But it has grown into a very important part of our coaching today at LSU.

Whether or not this was my invention doesn't make any difference because I don't think there are very many new things that have been invented in basketball. Probably a guy in Casper, Wyoming, in 1930 invented the four corners. Black universities were running the so-called motion offense years ago, but it didn't have a name. We Caucasians were saying they weren't disciplined because those schools didn't have their players running as robots or puppets the way we were doing it at the time. Now we're doing the same thing those black schools always did.

The psychology of having the Freak Defense can be a tremendous advantage. Years later, after I had come to LSU, we were getting ready to play Kentucky at Lexington. I was at the Lexington Marriott watching Eddie Sutton's television show. On the show they were interviewing Eddie and they asked, "Coach Sutton, you're getting ready for the LSU Tigers coming to town, what do you think?" "They're a tough team to prepare for," he said. "They play so many defenses when they use their freak defense that you really have to get your team accustomed." I've known Eddie for a long time and I knew how organized and categorical he was with his strategy. I called my assistant, Ron Abernathy, and I said, "We're not gonna play the Freak Defense against Kentucky. We're just gonna use it for only the first few minutes. 'Lo and behold, we beat them by 35 points for the worst defeat in the history of Rupp Arena.

After two years at Bishop Ryan, I was called into the army for the Berlin Crisis in 1961. I had signed up for the National Guard so that I could do my time without having to miss any of the school year. I could leave in the spring after basketball was over. But now I was drafted into the regular army. Ron

Erhardt took over the basketball team and off I went to Ft. Riley, Kansas. Football star Paul Hornung and I were in the same batallion together. I managed to make the time useful by becoming a player/coach for the Ft. Riley Engineers, and we went undefeated.

I came back to Minot and coached another three years at Bishop Ryan. I had no idea I wasn't making any money because I didn't know what it meant to make money. I think my salary at the end of five years was $6,500. Vonnie was teaching at Minot State Teachers College and we had a baby, Robyn. We could barely make ends meet. So we started asking ourselves if there was any future here in North Dakota. But it was our home—we didn't know anybody anywhere else and we loved what we were doing.

I went to see the administration about the money situation. I was concerned also that there was no teachers' retirement. I was informed that I was the highest paid coach on the staff. I felt almost greedy asking for more after that statement. One night after track practice, I was in the our coaches' office and something happened that changed our lives. All the coaches had Bishop Ryan letter jackets and we all hung them in the office closet. I came in ahead of everyone, showered, and was ready to go home. I grabbed a jacket, thinking it was mine. As I slid it on, something dropped out. I didn't remember having anything in my pocket. I picked it up, and saw it was a contract for the track coach, who hadn't been there as long as I had. He was making $900 more a year than I was; I couldn't believe it. So I went home and told Vonnie about it. I said, "That's wrong. I'm gonna quit." She didn't even think twice about it. She agreed with me.

I went to school the next day and informed the superintendent that I was leaving. That afternoon the president of the school board, Cy Butz, came to me. He was the Budweiser distributor in town. He said "Dale, I hear that you're leaving. Please don't leave us as we appreciate your work." He continued, "I hear you are unhappy. Well, I'll tell you what we're gonna do. You name your price and we're also going to get you your retirement plan. Just tell us what you need." I just looked at him and said "Nope." "What are you talking about?" he said. "I just gave you what you wanted." I said, "Nope, I'm leaving."

I went home and it was really Vonnie that said, "Let's pack our car with all of our belongings and go to California and get jobs." She had more guts than I did. That idea scared the heck out of me. Who did I know in California?

Just as I had done when I was suspended from the college basketball team eight years earlier, I went to Reuben Hammond and said, "Reuben, I'm really leaving this time. What do you think?" He said, "I'm fifty years old and I never left North Dakota. You're twenty-eight years old. You can go and are still young enough to always come back. I envy you." That sealed it.

Just as I was ready to leave North Dakota, Herb Parker pulled me aside. He said, "I want to tell you something. You've got a great future ahead of you in coaching, or whatever you do. But something that will always hold you back is you're quick on the fuse. You've got to keep that temper down." I never really listened to him. He was always a very nice man, but sometimes I almost thought he was too nice. As a result, I let it go in one ear and out the other. He was totally correct and there was no question about that. Had I listened and learned from his advice, had I been more mature, I would have saved myself a lot of pain along the way.

We made a little bed for Robyn in the back seat and took off for California. We didn't know a soul. We owned only one car so we both had to work in the same town. The first place we found two job openings was in Berkeley. There was a job as a teacher at Berkeley High School that Vonnie could have, and a job at a junior high school for me. It was the dawn of Mario Savio and the free speech movement. Rioters were tromping police cars and Haight Ashbury was in its heyday. I took the position at Garfield Junior High coaching the A and B teams and teaching physical education.

Berkeley at the time was a bedroom suburb for the rich and many of the professors at Cal-Berkeley. They were integrating for the first time; it was absolute chaos. Discipline was nonexistent in the school. It was an unbelievable experience. I told Vonnie every day when I left her at the high school, "Well, don't be surprised if I'm back here picking you up at noon. I'm going to get fired because I'm not going to listen to the rules that the administration has." They were totally against teacher discipline. They were just spineless. I was passing out padlocks the first day of class and all of a sudden I heard *thump, thump, thump.* I looked up and there are two kids with their shirts off, pummeling one another in rotation, hitting each other in the chest. I told them both, "Hey, knock it off and sit down." One kid looked at me and said, "Don't you point that finger at me." He was the biggest guy in the junior high. I walked over, grabbed him, and sat him down in the bleachers. One teacher asked me if I knew what the kids were doing. When I told him I didn't, he let me know they were "chesting." That's a game in the ghetto. You take off your shirt and you hit each other in the chest until you can't stand it anymore. The guy that I made sit down was known as "The Duke." He said, "That guy runs the school!"

The next day when I got to my office, there was the same kid, a good-looking kid who looked like Harry Belafonte, sitting in my office. He said, "Yeah, man, I'd like to talk to you." I said, "Well, first of all I ain't your man. Let's get that straight because I have no desire to talk to a punk." "What did you call me?" he said with an amazed look. "I said you're a punk. When you want to grow up, you come back and talk to me." So he took off. The next day he came back to my office. "Coach Brown, may I talk to you," he said a lot more politely. "Sure you can. Come on in." He came in and sat down and said, "Coach Brown, I'd like to be one of your squad leaders in physical education." I was appointing squad leaders to lead exercise. I said, "I'd be proud to have you as a squad leader. You came in today with a little better attitude and I'm going to put you in charge." "Well Coach, I'll tell you one thing. There won't be anybody late or out of uniform or mouthing off to you. You can be assured of that," he said. He had a big smile.

He and I became very close. He told me that his mother was white. She was from Nebraska. She ran away with a black carnival worker who had come to her small town. He felt he had to be tough so others wouldn't laugh at him. Sounded familiar, a lot like me. He wound up being a key guy for me because everybody in the school was afraid of him. He spread the word that everyone was to respect me.

One day a teacher came to me and said, "I've got a kid who is incorrigible." He was a little tiny guy. The teacher told me they were going to kick him out of school because no teacher would have him. I said, "Send him in to me." He came in and he was a wreck. You could tell he was a tough kid, he was all dirty and he looked tired. I sat him down and I said, "I know what it's like to be poor, but you don't have to be dirty. Look at your shirt. Look how dirty it is. Do you know that there are some people out there, now I'm going to be honest with you, that are going to call you a bum because of how you look? You don't want that to happen." I wanted to teach him a lesson I had learned early: people don't respect you if you don't respect yourself. So this tough kid started to get clean and really take pride in himself.

It was amazing how much different he looked a few days later. I asked him, "What's the thing you like to do the most?" He said he liked to play baseball. I asked him why he didn't go out for the team. "Because I don't have a glove," he said. "Willie, I didn't have a glove as a kid either, and that was really embarrassing. I would ask a kid from the other team to leave his glove in the field for me to use. But there were some kids who were stuck up and wouldn't let me use their gloves. So I understand. If you had a glove, would you play?" "Oh yeah," he said, jumping up. I promised him that during the next weekend I was going to pick him up and take him to buy a glove. I can still see him sitting there and staring at that glove. He started to cry. He asked me to write my name on it, and I said, "No, this isn't my glove. This is your glove." "I know, but I want your name on it," he said. "You're the first person to ever care about me." So I wrote my name on his glove. That, I guess, was my first autograph, and it means more than almost all the others I've ever signed.

The youngster didn't have a penny to his name, but at Christmas he brought a gift into my office. It was a rug that he had made for us. He actually made it in shop from different patches of carpet—red, green, gold, pink, yellow, blue. He had gone to the furniture stores and asked for scrap carpet. He sewed the scraps together and gave us this rug. It was the most beautiful thing, not because of how it looked but because of what it meant. All the teachers in the school were shocked that he had changed. The difference was that I not only cared for him, but I wouldn't take any crap from him. I wasn't scared of him because I didn't have an agenda. I didn't want anything from him. I think many teachers just had jobs. I have never had a job, I've had a career. That was the secret. I learned a lot from that year, but probably the greatest lesson was that if I treated young people with discipline, sprinkled with love, I had a real chance to make a difference. That's what does it.

That first Christmas, Vonnie and I didn't have any money at all. I did something that to this day I can't believe that I did. I borrowed several hundred dollars from one of those loan sharks near the Berkeley campus to buy Christmas gifts. It was a terrible experience, but fortunately I was able to pay him back—at an unbelievable interest rate.

I spent one year at Garfield and then I found an employment agency that helped me find another job. I knew I didn't want to stay at the junior high level, and it became clear to me one day when I was driving the team bus to a game. It's actually kind of funny. While I might not have been much of anything when I was coaching in North Dakota, at least I was president of the North Dakota Coaches' Association. At least a couple of my teams went to the state tournament. At least I was coaching at a high school. And now I was coaching at some inner city junior high. I really felt terrible about the direction my career was headed, and even for several years afterwards I never mentioned that I coached at a junior high. Now, I'm proud I did.

At any rate, I was driving the bus over to the game and it was raining. The kids were loud and rambunctious. Then suddenly all I could hear were the windshield wipers. It seemed like the sound of the wipers, the rhythm of the wipers, was chanting, "Dale Brown is a failure, Dale Brown is a failure, Dale Brown is a failure." I knew then, when the windshield wipers started talking to me, that I had to go find another job.

The employment agency came up with a couple of jobs. One of them was the head basketball coach in New Mexico, and the other was in Tigard, Oregon. I flew out to both and interviewed. I was offered both jobs, but Vonnie didn't want to leave California. That same day, I received a notice in the mail about a job opening in Palm Springs, California. I went for an interview and got the job. I was a high school head basketball coach again.

I took the job and was just shocked at how diametrically opposite Palm Springs was from Garfield Junior High. Because their parents were wealthy and influential, most of kids were absolutely disinterested in basketball. I wasn't there long before I realized that this was a dead end. I sat down and thought, "I'm not making any headway here in life, but where am I going to go?" I started writing letters to places where I thought I would fit in, where I would be comfortable. I eliminated the East Coast and put my efforts toward the West Coast and the Rocky Mountains. I sent a résumé to head college basketball coaches in those areas.

Ten percent wrote back. Of this 10 percent, I remember two guys in particular. The first was John Bennington from Michigan State, who wrote me a real nice letter encouraging me to never give up. I thought that was really nice of him, and I said to myself, "If I'm ever in a position where young coaches are writing me, that's what I'm going to do." To this day, I still do it. In fact, I end all my letters to those aspiring young coaches by saying: "Thanks for your interest in LSU and whatever you do, be certain to persevere because it is a most important ingredient in getting to the top."

I also got a letter from Ladell Anderson, the head coach at Utah State. I sent him another letter at Christmas, or if their team did well I'd send him a card congratulating him on big wins. I guess I made an impression because one weekend that next spring, I was at home when I got a telephone call. It was from Ladell Anderson. I almost had a heart attack. "Where are you, Ladell?" I asked. He said, "I'm in Palm Springs. I'm on my way to recruit a couple of junior college kids at Imperial Valley Junior College and I want to know if you will go with me." I said, "You want to know if I want to go with you? Of course!

Where are you?" He said he was at the gas station down the street at a pay phone. Before he could get the door to that phone booth open, I was there with my car to pick him up. We went to Imperial Valley Junior College where he was recruiting a junior college player of the year by the name of Shaler Halimon. Everybody wanted Shaler.

Imperial Valley is in the California desert. It was hotter than heck, seemed like 125 degrees in the shade. When Ladell and I pulled up, there was a guy working outside with this big old straw hat on and a rake. I rolled down the window. "Excuse me," I said, "do you know where we can find Shaler Halimon?" "I sure do," he said. "Right here, I'm Shaler Halimon." He was out raking leaves. I was caught off guard. I said, "This is Coach Anderson from Utah State and I'm Dale Brown!"

The conversation went real well with Shaler, and on the drive back Ladell said to me, "Would you be interested in coming to Utah State as my assistant?" I almost had my second heart attack of the day. I must have sounded like a kid. "Wow, I guess so," I said. He told me he could only offer $6,500. I said we probably couldn't make it on that, but that I would think about it. That was $4,600 less than I was making at Palm Springs. I asked if there was any way he could just go a thousand higher, and he said he didn't know. It was tough because I wanted the job so badly, but I had a family I had to think of. When we pulled into Palm Springs, he said, "Dale, you think it over and I'll call you." I talked it over with Vonnie and she agreed we should take it, even if it was just $6,500. Soon after, Ladell called me and said, "We can give you $7,500." I knew it was meant to be. "I'll take it," I said, trying not to yell. He said, "Well, your first mission is to recruit Shaler Halimon. You've met with him and know what to do." I really didn't know what to do, but I accepted the mission. For the next few weeks, I left the high school several afternoons near the end of my business class. Sometimes I even left business class early, telling them to check something out in their book, and then I took off for the highway to Imperial Valley.

The recruiting of Shaler Halimon was a real eye opener for me. I found him to be a great kid, and I'll never forget him as long as I live. I was a virgin in this profession. He didn't have anything, and he told me about all the offers he had from other colleges of cars and money and anything else he wanted. But he said, "I don't want any of that, Coach. I just don't want any of it." He continued, "I'll tell you what, I really like Coach Anderson and you. I would really like to go to Utah State." Well, I almost dropped dead. I thought this couldn't be that easy. I didn't even know if we had a good summer job for him. He said, "The only thing I would ask—and I don't want anything from anyone—is I've got a little bit of rent to pay, about $75. Do you know anyone I can borrow that $75 from?" I said, "Well I'll give it to you," never dreaming it was dishonest. I didn't give it to him that day because I didn't have it with me. When I got home, I called Ladell Anderson and told him Shaler said he was coming. "That's impossible," Ladell said. I replied, "That's not impossible, but he needs $75 to pay his rent, so can I just loan it to him?" "Oh no, you can't do that," Ladell said. "Why? I can't loan him $75 from my own money? I'm not giving him the money, I'm loaning it to him." Ladell explained to me that there was an NCAA rule prohibiting it.

I had never heard of such nonsense. I hung up the phone and I thought, now there's a decision I have to make. Do I start with my first recruit and cheat—and that's what it would be called, cheating—or do I lose this recruit because I was so honorable, and force him to go some other place he didn't want to go. Or do I try to beat the system. I said to myself, "I'm gonna beat the system." I got in touch with a businessman in Palm Springs. I told him that I would like him to meet Shaler.

I didn't say anything about a loan. Then I called Shaler and explained to him that I couldn't give him $75 because it was illegal for me to do. But I told him about this gentleman who wanted to meet with him. I didn't tell Shaler to ask him for anything. Shaler and the businessman met and he loaned Shaler $75. I gave the guy $75 back in case we lost track of one another.

Shaler signed with Utah State and became one of the greatest players in the school's history. After he graduated, he was the first round draft choice of the Philadelphia 76ers. Jack Ramsey came to Logan, Utah, to sign him. Shaler signed and got a $5,000 bonus. That very day he came into my office. I can still see him digging into his jeans and pulling out his money. He laid the money he borrowed on the desk and said thank you. I gave him a receipt and he ripped it up.

When I took the job at Utah State, I wasn't aware that part of the deal was that I was going to also be the head tennis coach. Maybe Ladell mentioned it to me, but I didn't remember it. As soon as the basketball season ended, the athletic director called me in and said, "You know you've got a tennis match next week." I said, "I've got what?" He replied, "You're the head tennis coach." I said, "I don't know one thing about tennis. I don't know how to score it. I've never played it in my whole life. How can I coach it?" My argument didn't get me anywhere with him. "Well, that's your job," he said. So I called a team meeting. I got all the guys together and I said, "Listen, I know nothing about tennis. I'm not going to learn about tennis. I have no interest in tennis, but I'll make sure you get the nicest uniforms and the best equipment. I'll get you in physical condition. You'll be on time and you'll be disciplined. But I am not about to be phony enough to make you think I can coach this game."

Our first trip was to play Arizona and Arizona State. I

47
●

think they were ranked No. 1 and No. 3 in the country. A guy from our sports information department came by my office and said it was my responsibility to call in the scores as soon as the matches were over. I got back to the hotel and called my top player in. "How'd you do?" I asked. "I lost 2–6, 3–6, 6–4, 4–6." I thought to myself, now is that 22 to 15, or what? Do you add the scores? So I went out to another player and asked, "Joe, how'd you do?" "6–zip, 6–zip, 6–zip." So we must have won 18 to nothing. I called another guy in and he gives me the scores in reverse. He said his score was 4–6, 4–6, 6–2, 6–3, 4–6. I thought now how in the heck can one guy have three scores and one guy have five? I didn't know the answer, so I didn't call the scores in. We got back on Monday, and the sports information director came in and asked why I didn't call the scores in. I didn't want to tell him the truth, so I said I forgot. I went to the library that day, checked out a book, and figured out how to keep score in tennis.

We wound up having the best won-loss record in the history of the Utah State University tennis team at that time, although the record has since been broken. The season ended and we turned in all our equipment. The next day I got a call from the head coach at the University of Montana. They were undefeated and were coming down to play in the Big Sky Conference Championship in Ogden, Utah. He said, "We'd like to have a match with your fine team. You've got about the best team out in the West." So I thought "Heck, there's another win." I told him, "Okay, come on." I got all the equipment out and got all the guys back. Montana showed up that weekend. I was walking around, standing by one of the matches, and the Montana State coach walked up to me. "Hi Coach! I'm impressed with how well your guys play the net. Do you use a lot of drills and stuff?" "Oh yeah, we sure do," I answered. I thought I'd better get out of there before he asked me to demonstrate one of the drills. I couldn't keep score, so how could I design any drills? "Yeah, we use a lot of drills," I said before I took off. I went to the next court and he followed me. "Damn, your number one singles guy gets a hell of a lot of velocity on his serve. Does that aluminum racquet help?" Aluminum racquet—I didn't know what the heck he was talking about. I thought all the racquets were made of wood. "Oh yeah, there's no question about that," I said. To make a long story short, we beat them 8–1. When a match is all over, you line up your tennis teams and everyone shakes hands. During the handshakes, the other coach said, "Can I just say something to all of you? This is by far the best-coached tennis team we have played." My guys were snickering out loud. They knew the truth.

While I was at Utah State, I had chances to get other jobs that were opening up, smaller head coaching jobs. But I never checked them out because I was always told by Ladell that if he ever left that I would be the head coach. During my second year there, I recruited a real scholar athlete out of Bishop Ryan back in Minot; a black gentleman who is today a lieutenant colonel in the air force. His father was a sergeant in the air force. His name was Sims Walker Jr. He was a good basketball player and an honor student. One day during his freshman year one of our administrators informed me that he needed to see me in his office.

I went into the administrator's office and he said, "About that boy of yours, Sims Walker. Are you aware that he's in the black student union?" There were twenty-three black students at Utah State out of nine thousand. That was the Black Student Union. It was simply a social club. He said, "I want him out of there today or he's getting pulled off scholarship." I went through the ceiling.

I said, "I'll tell you what, he isn't going to get out of that organization, and if you try to make him, I'll go to *Sports Illustrated* with this story." I turned and walked out of his office. I immediately found Ladell and told him what had happened. I said, "Ladell, this is absolutely wrong. It's wrong." Ladell agreed. Well, they never took his scholarship away, but I could tell that my relationship with some influential people there really changed for the worse.

I was just finishing my fifth season as Ladell's assistant and had taken two of our players to the Fellowship of Christian Athletes camp in Santa Barbara, California. When I checked into the dorm, there was an emergency message to call Ladell Anderson. I called and he said, "Dale, I think you should get back here right now. I have decided I'm going to take the coaching job with the Utah Stars." The Stars were the ABA team in Utah. Ladell said, "I'm going to give a double recommendation for you and Dutch Belnap." I asked him to repeat what he said, because I couldn't believe it. He had always told me I would be the next head coach at USU. I went in to see the athletic director and he also said I was going to get the job. But, curiously, he wanted me to fill out an application. He said that way it would really look good when I got the job. I went home and told my wife, "You are going to watch me end up on the short end of the totem pole. I'm telling you right now that I'm not getting the job. I know it, I can feel it."

The search committee brought in all kinds of people for an interview, but the whole time they were still telling me the job was mine. Then, the day they're going to announce the job, the athletic director called me to his house and said, "Dale, I've been in athletics twenty-five years. I've never met anyone who works harder, is a better recruiter or more honest. But I find it necessary to give the job to a man who has had some college head coaching experience. I'm going to give the job to T.L. Plain, the assistant at Kentucky who had been a head coach at

Transylvania University." I got up from my chair and I said to the athletic director, "Let me just say something. The only way you could have hurt my family more would have been to take me to midcourt at halftime and cut my guts out in front of ten thousand people in the arena. I quit." I walked out the door.

I went home and told Vonnie that I was finished with Utah State. The next day at the press conference, I stood there hurting badly. After the press conference, T.L. asked to meet with me. He said he wanted me to stay. I said, "Thanks, but I'm not interested in staying. I'm gonna resign." He asked where I was going to go. I said I didn't have a clue.

I got a call to visit the university president, who said, "Dale, you're a very valuable resource and we want you to stay here. We'd like to name you to a position in university relations." I said, "You have to be fooling. First of all, it's an insult. If you're afraid that I will bad mouth this university, I won't do that. I will have nothing but good things to say about this university. But I'm also not going to go out and recruit for a university that just cheated me out of a job. I'm not interested." I got up and walked out.

I had determined I was going to get out of coaching. I just wasn't political enough. I had left Minot because of a contract problem, and now I was supposed to have a job, but was suddenly cut out.

The next day, I got a call out of the clear blue sky from Bob Greenwood. He had just been hired as the head basketball coach at Washington State University. He wanted me to be his assistant. I realized that if I got out of coaching right then, everyone would believe I was a poor loser. Without really thinking about it, I said, "I'll take it."

My year at Washington State was one of the wildest rides of my life. It just never seemed to work out. There was a lot of friction on the team. At Christmas, the captain of the team came to see me. His name was Dan Steward, from Idaho. Dan said, "Coach, I'm the captain of the team, it's incumbent upon me to tell you that none of us are coming back after Christmas. We're gonna boycott the first conference game." I said, "I don't want to say anything about the coach, but let me say this to you. You owe this university, so save the university the embarrassment of boycotting, okay? You also owe Coach Greenwood. Don't destroy the man. I'm pleading with you to go talk to the guys and get them to come back." So he went and talked to them and they all came back.

We finished the season and then I resigned. Once again, I resigned and I had no job. It was the third job I had resigned with nowhere to go. The athletic director, Ray Nagel, called me into his office. He said, "I'm going to fire Bob Greenwood and I want to give you the head job." I said, "No way." He continued, "Well, I'm firing him tomorrow." The next day, Ray did as he said and he fired Coach Greenwood. Ray called me again to his house. "Okay, Dale, I'm going to make the announcement that I'm naming you head coach."

"No, you're not," I said. He asked why I was so insistent. I just told him, "Coach Greenwood gave me a job when I didn't have one. Things haven't gone so well this year, but if I took the head job, he would think I undercut him. I'm not going to have that. I'm not going to have anyone think I was disloyal."

At that moment I had no clue what I was going to do. But it didn't last long. I got a call that night from Carl Maddox, the athletic director at Louisiana State University. It wasn't long before I was off to Cajun Country and my big break as a college head coach.

4

The Influence of
the Wizard

One of the first things I did after accepting the job as head coach at LSU was call John Wooden, the legendary coach of UCLA. What he accomplished, winning ten NCAA championships, is unequaled. No one else ever dominated a sport like he did. Certainly, no one will ever do so again. He truly is the Rembrandt, the Michelangelo, the Leonardo da Vinci, the Einstein of basketball, all wrapped in one. He is the master.

The first time I met Coach Wooden was at the 1970 championship of the NCAA western regionals, playing for the right to go to the Final Four. Utah State was in the final eight, a feat considered impossible for Utah State. We played UCLA in the finals and were beaten. In 1971 I was at Washington State, and one of my duties was to scout our PAC opponents. As a competitor, our meetings were only casual.

As long as we were playing in his conference, I didn't feel

comfortable calling and asking for advice. Moving to LSU gave me the chance to ask for the opportunity to learn from the master, and just do nothing but pick his mind, hang around the office, and go to his house. He was so gracious. He never said, "I'm too busy" or "I don't have time."

He invited me to Los Angeles and welcomed me into his home like an old friend. He included me in his speaking engagements. He let me spend hours with him around his office. I took notes on everything. Prior to the visit, I made a lesson plan like a teacher uses in school. I started with A in the alphabet, and I thought about what was associated with basketball that began with the letter A that I could learn from this man. I wrote "academics, attitude and ability." Then I went to B: bulletin boards, what do you do with your bulletin boards? How do you best use boxing out techniques? The letter P was psychology. I asked him to explain his psychology. I didn't want to miss anything. I had pages of questions and he answered every one of them.

I end most of my coaching clinics by telling the story of the last day I was there visiting John Wooden. He and his wife, Nell, walked me to my car. John put his arm around me and said, "Dale, I really enjoyed spending time with you. But I could have saved you a lot of time if I'd just told you my secrets of coaching." I practically broke my neck trying to get my pen and pad out in time to scribble this down. I thought this was really going to do it for me. He said, "One, make certain that you always have better players than the team you play; two, make sure those players put the team above themselves; and three, a very important point, always practice simplicity with constant repetition, and you will be successful."

The longer I've coached, the more I've grown to realize how right he was. It has gotten tougher and tougher over the years to do all those things, but those still remain the rules for putting together a winning program.

I also spent time with Adolph Rupp at Kentucky that same summer. Besides basketball, he taught me about working with the media, disciplining players, and handling pushy parents. Both of those men became grandfather figures to me. They both accepted me, I never pushed my way in.

To this day, I talk to Coach Wooden several times a month. I teach my team about his pyramid of success. When our team goes to the West Coast, I usually try to get John to talk to the players. He is an inspiration.

I would say that Coach Wooden was one of the seven men in my life from whom I really learned, and for whom I have undying respect. I respect Father Hogan, Reuben Hammond, and Herb Parker back in Minot. I respect Tex Winter, who is now an assistant to Phil Jackson of the Bulls. I respected Norman Vincent Peale, the father of positive thinking. And I have a great deal of respect for Bob Richards, the former Olympian who is such a dynamic public speaker. What makes these men special is that each taught me more about life than basketball.

Perhaps the most special trait of Tex Winter is his unselfishness. When I was a high school coach and he was coaching at Kansas State, I wrote him a letter. He was hot; everyone in the country wanted him. He was the coach of the year. His team was in the Final Four and ranked number one in the nation. In this letter I told him I wanted to come and learn basketball from him. He was fantastic. He took me to his home to eat, took me to the country club to eat, stayed up late at night, watched multitudes of films, and talked to me one on one. I really learned a lot. I learned practice organization from him. He knew how to pull practices together, and that's truly a skill. Just to have practice for the sake of practice doesn't mean anything, just to have drills to have drills doesn't mean anything. It's all a sequence and it takes a lot of time. You can't believe the hours we put into practice planning alone at LSU, making sure we have a master plan.

As I watched everything Tex did, it was easy to see it come together. It was like a puzzle. And he had no ego whatsoever. He and John Wooden were clearly the biggest influences on my coaching career.

Then there are the two people that kept my spirits up for many years. I had not actually met either one of them until after I took the job at LSU: Norman Vincent Peale and Bob Richards. I had every tape, every film that Bob Richards had ever made; and I had every book that Norman Vincent Peale wrote, and every quote that he ever said all the way back from when I was in high school. It's kind of funny, but I believed, even when I was in high school, that one day I would meet both of them.

In 1973, Norman Vincent Peale came to Baton Rouge for a big convocation in the LSU Assembly Center. I had just finished my first year at LSU. I mentioned to one of the people who was organizing the speech that I would love to go and meet him backstage. I was actually nervous. I went to his dressing room, and he was there with his wife. It was unbelievable. We sat there for almost an hour and had the greatest talk. The next day there was a story about Norman's speech in the Baton Rouge paper. He was quoted saying, "I had the opportunity to meet the new head basketball coach, Dale Brown, in my dressing room; and if I wasn't motivated before then, I certainly was after meeting him." I thought "Wow! He said *I motivated him.*"

Later he came back and made a prediction that LSU would win a national championship. That was quite an honor coming from the father of positive thinking.

The Influence of the Wizard

I clipped the quote from the paper and I wrote him a letter. I said that I was absolutely thrilled to have had the opportunity to meet him, that I had read every book he had written, and that he had kept my spirits up when nothing else could. I thanked him for the wonderful things he said about me and the team to the media. And I asked him to keep in touch, which he did. I'd call him, he'd write me. We became good friends. Then in 1985, we decided to make a motivational video just for the team. In that film I wanted Norman Vincent Peale and John Wooden to speak. They both agreed. In that film, Dr. Peale repeated his belief that there was no question LSU would win a national championship. No question whatsoever. In 1992, I got a call from some folks who were writing a book on his life, asking me to write the foreword. I just couldn't say enough about him.

What hit home with me most about Norman was his knowledge of the abilities of the subconscious. Before anyone even knew about the subconscious, Norman discovered its importance through his spiritualism. He was very similar to Billy Graham, never a scandal associated with either of them. More than fifty years ago, Norman Vincent Peale was trying to tell people about the power of the subconscious, but they didn't want to listen. He was rejected for his beliefs. He explained that before most people are thirteen years old, they have been told "no, no, no, no" 180,000 times. No one ever stimulates with positive things. As a result, most of the things people think about themselves are negative. He was right when he commented that you can walk in a room and be critical and no one will notice. But if you walk in a room and say, "Boy, it's a great day. I love you all. Have a nice day," everyone will say when you leave, "What the hell's wrong with that psycho?" He even took it a step further by showing that you become what you think, and that the mind has more power than the body.

But the most beautiful thing about Dr. Peale was that he was absolutely, one hundred percent real.

During the fall of 1993, I was invited to participate in a dinner and a video presentation honoring Dr. Peale's life. It was an honor to be a part of such an inspirational event. When Robyn and I arrived in Nashville for the dinner, they announced that Dr. Peale couldn't make it due to a travel problem. Something told me I would never see him again; I knew he wasn't in the best of health. That's why I really wasn't shocked, though I certainly was sad, when I learned that Dr. Peale passed away in January 1994. What we lost was more than just an advocate of positive thinking. We lost a national resource. If there are such things as saints, he was one. He had it all, he was positive, he was loving, he was free of ego, shy to the point that he almost had an inferiority complex. I think he'll go down in history as one of the most prominent men associated with helping others. Norman had a philosophy of life. Ask God for forgiveness and he'll give it to you. Fairly simple, huh? We lost one of the great men in history. He touched more lives than any of us will ever realize.

My friendship with Bob Richards occurred around the same time as my relationship with Dr. Peale. He was a decathlon champion and an Olympic pole vault champion. In 1973, he came to Baton Rouge to speak at our basketball banquet. I knew there was a lot I could learn from him. All of Bob's stories were about failure, hanging in there, and overcoming the belief that things just couldn't be done. They were sports stories, so they really hit home with me. He touched on topics like injuries, and people who were cut from teams. One memorable story was about Mark Spitz, the Olympic swimmer. His first trip to the Olympics was a miserable failure. At the end of those games he said to himself, "The next time I'm going to get seven world records and seven gold medals." He did exactly what he said he was going to do. Spitz programmed himself for success.

The best part of Bob's visit, though, was how he spoke. He was dynamic, had an excellent vocabulary, wonderful analogies. I patterned myself after him, knowing that someday I would like to help people by speaking that way. I sometimes feel like I'm the greatest plagiarist in history because I took so many speaking ideas from Bob Richards.

5

Paper Tigers

I never really wanted to coach in the South. All I remember growing up and during my early days in the business was that the South was still very prejudiced. I had a jaundiced opinion based solely on what I had read in books. To me, the Deep South was James Clark from Selma, Alabama—his foot up on the bumper of a pickup, a shotgun in one hand and a cigar in the other, hosing down and beating blacks, or turning dogs on them. I got the call from LSU's athletic director Carl Maddox, and he asked if I was interested in the job as head basketball coach. He had his selection down to five head coaches and five assistants, and I was one of the assistants he wanted to invite for an interview. He asked me to fly to LSU.

I went in and told Ray Nagel, the athletic director at Washington State, that I was going to interview for the LSU job. He asked me to call him before I accepted any offer.

During my interview, I told the search committee what I would do to turn the program around. I said, "I think you should know before you interview me that I am not going to be dictated by a kid's ethnic status, color, or religion. I'm recruiting human beings first and basketball players second. It makes no difference to me what they look like. That's the way I operate." Afterwards, I called Vonnie from a pay telephone and told her about making that comment during the interview. I was on my way to a state tournament up in Alexandria, Louisiana. She said, "You'll never get that job. You would have had a much better chance of being a kamikaze pilot in the Japanese air force than getting that job." When they did not call for a few days, it appeared she might be right.

The one thing I remember most about that first trip to LSU was the beautiful campus. It was like a gingerbread land, it was like the Garden of Eden. I always wondered where the Garden of Eden was. It was supposed to be in Iraq somewhere, but I was convinced this was it. The arena was brand new—in its first year. It was clean and spacious.

I got a call about a week later asking if I would bring Vonnie down for a second interview. We went, and to my surprise, they offered me the job. As promised, I called Ray Nagel and told him I was offered the job, but I hadn't made a decision yet. LSU had given me two hours to make the decision. I told Ray I felt I should take the job and that I would appreciate it if he didn't make the decision any harder by trying to talk me out of it.

I found out later that I was offered the job only after they had first offered it to Bob Boyd, the head coach at USC. As Bob was getting on the airplane to leave, he told Carl Maddox he wasn't interested in the job. He suggested they interview me. Bob was one of two people who mentioned my name to Carl. The other was Joe Dean, who was then with Converse.

Joe Dean told me, "If you take the job, you will raise the flag, you will sing the national anthem, you will keep your own stats, and you will sweep the floor. They are totally uninterested in basketball." I did not know how right he was until our first practice. I went downstairs an hour and a half before practice and the baskets were not up. The court was dirty. I went upstairs and said, "How can we start practice like this?" The answer I got was, "Oh, we start basketball practice today?" I had to sweep and mop the floor with my own managers. We had to get Windex and clean the backboards. Yet, if the freshman practice football field had one blade of grass that was tilted sideways, they sent ten trucks and 162 men out there to straighten it. That is the way it was when we started.

I had a lot to learn about Louisiana when I got here. My first week on the job I was working late at night in the office with my assistant, Jack Schalow. I was going through the mail when I opened a letter from a guy that said, "I saw you on television last week and I want to tell you you're a real coon ass." I wadded it up and threw it over at Jack and said, "Look at that. You think I'm gonna get intimidated here? That's a bunch of bull."

A day or so later I was in Carl Maddox's office and he asked how things were going. I said, "Carl, I'm gonna tell you right now, no one's gonna intimidate me. They rang the wrong doorbell if they're trying to scare me." He asked what happened. "Well, I got some letter from some racist. He said he saw me on television when I was being interviewed in New Orleans. I told the interviewer that I was gonna recruit human beings first and basketball players second. Well this guy wrote me and he called me a coon ass."

Carl started to laugh and I said, "I don't think it's funny at all, Mr. Maddox." He started laughing even harder and said,

"Do you know what a coon ass is? It is a slang name for our wonderful cajuns." Man, I was embarrassed.

I have said that my mother was the most pathologically honest person I have ever met. Carl Maddox is second. He reminded me of my North Dakota upbringing. He always gave me 100 percent support. And it was a tough job for Carl because no one had built a basketball program at LSU. There had been fleeting moments of greatness like the days with Bob Pettit and Pete Maravich.

Carl was just so honest. He was really blunt and that is one reason I loved him. I learned to truly admire him late one afternoon as we were leaving his office. It was about 5:30, and we were talking about an assortment of issues. Suddenly, a man came charging up towards the athletic department. He walked up rather arrogantly. Carl said, "How are you, Senator?" Carl was a real southern gentleman. "I want you to meet our new head basketball coach, Dale Brown," Carl said. The Senator didn't really seem to care. I expected him to at least welcome me to Louisiana. Instead, he just started in, "Mr. Maddox, I want to show you something." He took some tickets out of his pocket. "You see these football tickets, I'm not pleased with them at all. I don't like where they're located and I expect them to be changed next year. Do you understand, Mr. Maddox?" Carl took the tickets, removed his glasses, slid out his pen and said, "Senator, I will make certain that these tickets are changed next year." I thought for a minute I had made a wrong decision about Carl, and how strong he was. Then Carl said, "I'm certainly glad you notified me of this, Senator. Let's see . . . these tickets are in section R. Your tickets will be in section Z next year. I can promise you that. Thank you, Senator." Carl handed the tickets back and walked away. Wow, I could have hugged him! Carl wasn't the kind to be intimidated and I will never forget it. He is a wonderful man, and how he had the guts to hire a no-name guy like me is really something.

The job was considered impossible, and most people were not interested in it due to the dominance of the football program. A local writer from the afternoon paper made a statement after I was hired: "Dale Brown inherited a job that, if it's not impossible, it's as close to impossible as any college basketball job in this country."

The entire salary was only $23,000. That might have been a problem for some people who may have otherwise been interested. It was not a problem for me. I mean, I did not even ask what my salary was. I never asked the salary until I signed a contract. I only owned three suits and a Volkswagen when I took the job. I had $800 in cash, that was it. We had nothing else to our name.

But I saw the fact that this was not the best basketball job as an advantage. You didn't have to win, because they hadn't won in the past. They had four winning seasons in the eighteen years prior to my arrival. To me, it was a challenge. I would not be good at going in to coach a team that had traditionally been on top. That wouldn't even be a challenge. I guess that's always been part of my nature. I get bored very easily with things. I need a challenge to stimulate me. I'd much rather try to win where you shouldn't and survive where they said you couldn't. Twenty-three years later, here I am. That is what is amazing.

There certainly had been some great players at LSU. And probably the greatest player was Pete Maravich. Pete had some very negative feelings toward the university because he felt his father, who I replaced, had been treated badly in the end. Plus Pete had been suspended from school for missing classes after finishing his career. But Pete's negative feelings gave me the chance years later to have a great conversation with him. We were playing Oklahoma at Oklahoma City and he was doing television color for the game. The night before the game, we were eating and he came over and tapped me on the shoulder. I invited him to sit down. We had a glass of iced tea and I said, "Pete, we haven't had a relationship, but will you come and talk to the team?" He agreed, and it was one of the best speeches I have ever heard.

He started out with, "None of you are going to be on the cover of *Sports Illustrated* as many times as me. I've been on it five times. None of you are going to break my scoring record. I'm the leading scorer in the history of college basketball." About this time I was beginning to wonder where this speech was headed. He continued,

None of you are going to have as much success in the NBA as I did. I was an all-star. I drove a Lamborghini and a Rolls. I bought mansions in every city that I lived from Atlanta to New Orleans to Boston. I have taken every kind of drug imaginable. I used to walk around with three thousand dollars cash in my pocket all the time because I loved to gamble. I thought happiness was lots of money and possessions. One night I climbed up on the roof of my house in Covington, Louisiana, and tried to communicate with people from outer space. That night I made up my mind to commit suicide. I was going to get a gun, put it in my mouth, and pull the trigger. But at that moment, I thought I'd try just one more thing. I fell on my bed crying and I said, "If there's a God, then please help me." I don't know what it was but something hit me. I just want to tell you that all of those things I thought would bring me happiness did not. I was a miserable human being until four years ago when I took God into my life. So don't let the basketball control you. When I took God it was the first true happiness I have ever had in my life.

It was beautiful. I think the team was shocked. They went from thinking he was bragging to really respecting him. And I learned as much as they did. It reiterated what I had been taught all my life. I knew one should not be controlled by possessions, but it also made indelible to me the fact that fame is fleeting, it is artificial, it is really meaningless in the end. Look at all Pete had, and he was going to take his own life.

Without a player like Pete, I had to try anything to get people interested in LSU basketball. I kept imagining what I could do to promote the game, because I knew it would take time to get good players to come. "I have to let people know we are here. I have to attract people somehow."

My very first idea was to buy purple and gold basketball nets. I found a company in Korea that manufactured purple and gold nets. I had my assistant's wife, Janet Drew, who was pretty good at poetry, write a poem about LSU basketball: "This is a net from the purple and gold for a sport that will never grow old." We decided to call our quest for the top a safari—a Tiger Safari. I got some plastic sacks and put the purple and gold nets in them along with my business cards. I put schedules in there too.

We headed out to all parts of the state and anytime we would spot a basket we would knock on the door and say, "I'm the basketball coach at LSU and I would like to give you this net." *Sports Illustrated* picked it up and wrote an article. I think it was the first time there was anything about us in a national magazine.

We also had wild halftime entertainment. We had the House of Representatives play the Senate in a game. We had all the LSU alumni doctors play the alumni lawyers in a game. We had the mayor and the governor referee the halftime entertainment. We had all kinds of contests. At Thanksgiving, I bought a bunch of pot holders and sent them to people who supported us. The pot holders said *"Thanks* for *giving* your support to LSU basketball." I bought coin purses with our logo and gave them to anyone who would listen. You would not believe the ideas we came up with just to promote the game.

My first team was predicted to win two games and finish in the cellar of the Southeastern Conference. The year before the team finished close to the cellar in the SEC and had a losing season. The team we inherited had very little talent, and we knew we needed some desperately. One day I was in the post office mailing boxes for Vonnie, and I happened to look over at a wanted poster. That's a great idea, I thought. I'm going to make a wanted poster and put a team picture on it. Underneath the picture it will say, "You are wanted at the following games. Come and see Smarty Marty Allman and Wild Bill Whittle. You be the judge. These guys will steal your heart. We want 14,351 jurors in attendance."

The guys on the team actually started to develop their identity from that poster. The nickname that was given to the team was the Hustlers. As promised, they did capture everybody's heart. It all began with our very first home game. We were playing Memphis State, ranked third in the nation. To everyone's surprise, we beat the daylights out of them. We won 94–81. That same Memphis State team went on to play UCLA for the NCAA championship at the end of the year. We won fourteen games, pulled off some major upsets with nationally ranked teams and went 9–9 in the SEC. We wound up in fifth place in the league. I was named the SEC coach of the year and was a candidate for national coach of the year. Everything just fell into place.

Tiger in a Lion's Den

After that fourteen-win season, Al McGuire, the coach at Marquette, was in Baton Rouge for a coaching clinic. He said to me, "Boy, you made a mistake." I asked, "Why?" "Well," he said, "you won fourteen games with no talent, and now next year they will want you to win twenty games. It is a game of high expectations. You're supposed to build it up slowly, win six games, eight, ten, twelve. That looks good." I laughed. Well, that's just about what happened. Two of the next three years we were a game away from being .500. We were 12–14, 10–16 and 12–14.

The last home game that I coached during my fourth year—which followed three losing seasons—a group of students stood up when I came out on the court and hollered, "Hey Brown, who's gonna be sitting in your wife and daughter's seats next year?" My assistant, Rob Abernathy, took off toward them. I grabbed him by the arm and said, "Well, we'll get the last laugh so let's just calm down. Someday, when we turn this around, they'll be begging for tickets." I wonder where those students are today.

Our biggest problem was we could not convince black players to come to LSU. It seemed that LSU was the last school in the SEC to integrate its basketball program. Maybe there was a school in Albania that had fewer blacks than LSU, but I doubted it. They had one black player in the history of the school, and that was the year before I arrived. Most blacks didn't want to come because they thought there was racism. Many of the black kids were told they could not make it academically. And they didn't want to come to a school that hadn't won in a long time.

I came to LSU at a time when cheating was more rampant than ever. There were lots of ways to cheat that did not involve cash payments. I would get a kid's official high school transcript, and realize that he could not get into LSU. The next thing I knew, he had been admitted into a competing school that had standards at least as high as ours. I knew he could not be eligible—I had his transcript. Yet nothing was done. I know of an incident where one player had six different transcripts. There was a coffee stain on one corner of the original transcript, but it was not on several of the other versions. It was all so tricky. One of his high school teachers had died, and someone changed the records of his grades in her classes all the way back to the ninth grade. By giving him all *A*'s in her classes, they were able to make him eligible.

There also was the problem of trying to build a basketball program at a football school. There were many people who wanted me and the basketball program to fail, who had no desire to help at all. There were an awful lot of people who believed in football and spring football, and that was it.

We had incidents where our guys had to get in the back of the meal line while a hundred football players went ahead of them. They were asked in the line, "Are you a football player?" If you said no, you would get spaghetti and meatballs or a tiny four-ounce steak. If you said yes, you would get a big steak. One time in particular, I had a late practice. Afterwards, I sent the team to the dining hall for dinner, then had a meeting planned later in the evening. The players all came wandering into the meeting late, and I was irate. I asked them why they were late and they answered, "Coach, we're really sorry. The football team came in and they made us all wait in line behind them. That's why we're late." I was very upset and that never happened again.

We did not even have a pep band for basketball. Thank God for a guy named Dr. Charlie Roberts. Out of the kindness of his heart, he started a group called the Court Jesters. Charlie Roberts did it all himself. My assistant coach, Jack Schalow, and I conducted the first tryouts for dancing girls.

There were no dancing girls for basketball. We went around the campus and encouraged the coeds to try out.

When our team traveled commercially, we would drive to New Orleans to catch the plane. One of the custodians or grounds people at the school would drive the bus. The very first time we took the bus, there was no heat and the bus hadn't been cleaned since the turn of the century.

There was no television show about LSU basketball until Jim Talbot helped me get one started. In 1978, I asked if we could start a television show. The answer was "No, that's impossible. You can never have a television show. No one will support it." "I'll tell you what," I said. "I'll get it going for two or three weeks and then you can take it over." They all laughed until Jim pulled it off.

There were two radio stations that carried LSU basketball. Only two radio stations! We have fifty now. The newspaper coverage was nonexistent. There were thirty-five days from the first day we practiced until the first game with Memphis State, and LSU basketball was seldom even mentioned in the local newspaper. When I brought it up to the media, one columnist was very offended for my daring to point it out.

Even simple things, like our media guides, were not done on time. We would go to the conference preseason media day and only two schools would never have their media guides available. LSU was one of them. So I decided to get people at LSU to do what was needed. "I'm going to get them to think that I'm about half-lunatic. I am walking straight over to the Sports Information office and I'm going to get mad and I'm going to make them think, 'What's he going to do next?'" Sometimes it is good to have people think that way, but I would never do it again. It took so much energy just to work with my own university. Forget about the energy it took to play Kentucky and the other college basketball powers.

We were lucky if we could recruit anybody to fill the roster. People just weren't interested in LSU basketball. How could they be? For example, I was in Shreveport recruiting this youngster. His mother said, "We can't come down there for every game." I said, "That's no problem. Maybe you couldn't come down for every game, but you certainly could listen on the radio." She laughed. "You can't listen to LSU basketball on the radio. There isn't a station we can pick up that broadcasts the games." I couldn't believe it. So when I returned to Baton Rouge, I went to Sports Information and asked if she was right. They told me that you could not pick up the LSU basketball games outside a hundred mile radius.

A funny thing happened after my fourth season at LSU. I got a call from the folks at Utah State. They were calling to offer me a job as both the athletic director and the head basketball coach. I said no, but that I'd really like it if Utah State would come play us. They accepted a few years later. We beat them by 32. I enjoyed it.

While we were close to .500, those first four seasons were not fulfilling. At the end of the fourth year, I was not sure about my future. I was aware that there was cheating going on in college sports, but Utah State had not been in the big time, so I didn't really notice it. Now I was in the big time. Honestly, the cheating depressed me.

My first real eye-opening case involved a top recruit we had a chance to sign. First of all, I didn't think he was that good. But when I arrived with my assistant, Jack Schalow, for the visit at his home, there was an agent there. We were eating chocolate cake when the agent said to me, "Coach Brown, if this young man decides to drive back and forth from school to home, how does he get new tires if he has a blowout? How are those paid for?" I played dumb. "I don't know. I guess you go to a wholesaler." "So Coach," he asked, "what's the rule on tickets?" "You can get four tickets," I answered. "Well, what if we need twenty tickets?" he continued. "I don't think they sell out at LSU," I answered. I was trying to be nice, but it was easy to see what was happening.

Jack and I got in the car and Jack said, "What's that all about?" I said, "It stinks, that's what it's about. This guy is trying to manipulate us. I smell this thing a mile away." A week later, I got a call from the player's father. He said the family was coming to Baton Rouge for the LSU–Notre Dame football game. I got the family some tickets through the athletic department but they were up in section U. My assistants and I had seats on the fifty-yard line at the time, so I told my one assistant coach to give them one of his tickets and I'll give them my two. I would just sit in the press box. We mailed them three tickets on the fifty-yard line. It was an afternoon game, one of the biggest in LSU history. Just before the game, Jack and I were walking across the street to the stadium and we bumped into the kid's parents. I spoke to them as they walked ahead of us. "How are you doing," I said to his father. I can still see him reaching in his shirt pocket and pulling out those tickets. He said, "I'm just not too sure how I'm doing." I thought maybe I had mailed them the wrong tickets. I said, "Those tickets are right on the fifty-yard line." I didn't tell him they were my tickets. He answered, "That's not the problem. Last week my son visited another school and I didn't have any trouble getting fourteen tickets. Now at LSU I can only get three tickets." I handed him his tickets back and I said, "Whoa, if that's the way you're going to judge a school, then I think you should send your son to that other school." I walked across the street and Jack Schalow said, "I guess that means we won't be recruiting him anymore, huh?" I answered, "You are right." And I never called him again. He went to one of our rivals.

Combined with my losing record, what I was learning

about all the cheating really had me worried. I went to see Carl Maddox and the chancellor, Paul Murrill. I said to them both, "I feel bad about coming here to see you, but I don't want to create any problems. I'm just not sure I can get the job done with my philosophy." They looked at me and asked what I meant by that. I said, "I'm not going to run out and change transcripts and get slush fund monies. But if we don't, we may lose a lot." Carl Maddox just stared at me and said, "You continue to do the job exactly like you're doing it. Show the discipline that you're showing, and I'll back you a hundred percent." That really relaxed me, it made me realize that they were in my corner.

The following year we had a winning season. That was our breakthrough. From there, it went uphill quickly.

Right after I had taken the job at LSU, I sat down with a pen and paper and decided to list my goals. I kept the list in my desk. About six years ago, I pulled it out and added a few more. The thought grew out of a conversation I was having with some friends about their coaching goals and their personal goals. I decided to ask myself, what are my goals?

My personal goals were to be the best father and husband I possibly could. Be the best human being I could. Be the best coach I could. Try to make the world a better place to live in. Keep my faith. Be thankful for all my blessings. Keep my body in good condition. Never take advantage of anyone. Never be scared. Control my ego. Be honest. Admit my mistakes. Never hold a grudge. Display my love. Help others. Be careful of being taken advantage of. Don't waste time. Don't be self-conscious. Put God first. Forget personal mistakes and don't look back, or feel guilty or unworthy of God's or others' love. Don't talk so much. Be a better listener. Don't try to impress anyone. Don't compromise what is right. Develop each player to his fullest capacity on and off the court. Be confident. Don't panic. Don't lose my temper. Don't let the critics bother me. Be fair to assistants and everyone that I work with. Be strong, firm, fair, consistent. Never think negatively, but be realistic. Never be inferior to anyone or envious in any way. Be firm but professional with officials and respect their difficult job. Try to improve officiating. Never embarrass anyone, talk about them or blame them. Forget the game after I analyze it. Don't be a martyr. Relax and have fun. Don't be nervous. Love those in our basketball family, but firmly display discipline. Always be honest. Respect others' decisions. Don't be afraid of results after using my head, heart and soul. Now I have a new one: Be the best grandfather I can be for Christopher Brown Prud-homme.

When I read over these, I sometimes think, "Boy, you ain't making much headway."

6

Turning It Around

Though there was an abundance of seats available at the assembly center when we took over, that changed as we started turning things around. And while it felt then like it took forever to get things moving upwards, the truth is we started creating excitement in the first five years.

My good friend Jim Talbot has told me that he and several of his friends really thought about coming out to see us after a game we played in Kentucky in 1976. It was a game we lost, but the stories that grew out of it drew a lot of attention.

When we played against Kentucky we never got a break. This particular game is a perfect example of what it was like. LSU had never beaten Kentucky at Rupp Arena, but we were leading and it looked like we had a real good chance of breaking that string. One of our best players, Kenny Higgs, was from Kentucky. He was runner up for Mister Basketball in

Kentucky. Anyway, Kenny was headed for a breakaway layup and a Kentucky player tackled him. It was clearly an intentional foul. I mean a fight almost broke out. The referees were trying to figure what to call. Is it intentional? Who gets kicked out? How may free throws does Higgs get? Does the basket count?

One referee had the ball in his hand and an assistant coach from Kentucky walked right over and punched the ball out of his hand. I can still see Joe Hall as he took his game program in one hand and slapped it hard against his other hand. He shouted, "That's bull what you're gonna do." So I walked over to where the referees were standing with Joe. Remember, I'm still a rookie, but I walked over and said, "What's going on?" The referee just looked at me and said, "Go sit down."

As I walked back toward our bench, I could not believe just because Joe has a big name and I have no name, the referee was afraid of him but not me. Boy, I was not going to let this happen. So I headed back there again and he told me to sit down again. I told the referee, "I'm not gonna sit down." To make a long story short, I got the technical and then they fouled practically our whole team out by the end of the game. I had no one left to put in the game. There was two and a half minutes to go. I had my last man in there and by that time it was obvious we were going to lose. Joe still had his first team in.

I said to myself, "You know what's happening here? It's the same thing that happened to my mother. She was in a bad spot, yet she couldn't speak up. She had to take that welfare worker's stuff, she had to take that hard time from the landlady. I am not taking this." So I called a timeout and walked over to the referee as calmly as I could. I took my coat off and I tapped him on the shoulder. I wasn't trying to get a technical, but I said, "Hey, I just want you to look over on my bench. We had a 12-point lead when this whole thing fell apart. I want you to look at my guys over there heartbroken." He just rolled his eyes and said, "What about it, Coach?" He was trying to be kind of smart. I told my assistant to take the huddle and I went back to the referee and said, "What about it? It's very simple. You've broken their hearts because this game has totally gotten out of hand. You and I both know that's not fair." I took off my coat and I said, "You've taken everything away from us. I've had all my starters foul out. I've got no one left to put in the game, so you might as well have a part of my wardrobe too. Here, take my sports coat." He looked at me like I was crazy and he said, "Oh no, I am not taking it." I said, "No, please take it. You've got everything else."

He turned his back to me so I thought I should make an impression on this guy. He's going to remember this, and maybe the next time he'll give us a break. "Well, if you won't take my coat, I'll tell you what I'm going to do. I'm taking it and I'm throwing it out right in the middle of that court." He waved his hand at me and said just go sit down. When he said "go sit down" like I was a junior high coach, I took off toward center court where Kentucky had a great big blue letter K painted right in the middle. I took off my sports coat and spun it around on my finger like a propeller and let it fly. It twirled around in the air and then floated down just perfectly on top of that K, completely covering it up. The Kentucky fans went nuts. Back home, people like Jim Talbot heard about it and decided they had better come out and get a look at this team.

I really felt it was what I had to do at the time. Pretend you are a referee. Dale Brown comes in the league. Who is Dale Brown? He is just a guy from North Dakota. The weak referees were not ever going to give me a break, and there were some very very very weak officials in this league at one time.

In retrospect, there were an awful lot of things which I did with a little more flair than I wished. It would have been nice to have the luxury of simply folding up a program, crossing my legs and sitting like John Wooden. I knew if I sat like that I'd get cold-cocked. I wanted some people to be uncomfortable because being nice wasn't getting me anything but a dirty floor, baskets that were not rolled out on time, a press brochure that was late and bad calls from bad referees. Many times I would have loved to have been more reserved and I'd love to have been sensitive. But there sometimes comes a point in your life, like Pat Riley said in his book, where you have to dig in and kick ass. It isn't any fun to do, but if you don't do it you will be devoured.

Three other games against Kentucky were very important in our developing a national program. The first was a loss in my third season. Kentucky just killed us. They beat us by 35 points, 115–80. It was the worst I had ever felt after a basketball game. I told friends after that game that, like MacArthur, I'd be back. Well, it took eleven years, but we beat Kentucky in 1986 by 35 points, 76–41, and it was the worst loss Kentucky had ever had at Rupp Arena.

Maybe one of the biggest wins ever for our program was also against Kentucky. It happened in 1978, our sixth season.

The Wildcats came to Baton Rouge ranked number one in the country. This was a team starring Rick Robey and Jack Givens, who went on to win the national championship. This was a tremendous Kentucky team. When they arrived in Baton Rouge, they had suffered only one loss. We were playing very well, taking as much as a 12-point lead. But then, just like before, it all started falling apart.

Before the game was over, all five of our starters had fouled out. Still, we tied them and the game went into overtime. Then with less than two minutes to go in the overtime,

Jordy Hultberg, who now is a television sportscaster in Baton Rouge, hit a jumpshot that gave us a 90–89 lead. We held on and ended up winning 95–94.

That game was unbelievable. Suddenly, everyone believed we were for real. We finished 18–9 that year.

That game was a key building block for our move onto the national scene. The next year, with DeWayne Scales, Rudy Macklin, Lionel Green, Jordy Hultberg, Greg Cook, Willie Sims and Ethan Martin, we won our first SEC regular season championship in twenty-five years. And just two years later, everyone knew who LSU was. That was the year we went 26–6, won our first SEC tournament championship, and made it to my first ever Final Four.

I believed we were destined to win the 1981 national championship. We won 31 games that year, the most in the country. We had a 26-game winning streak, the longest in the country. We went through the NCAA tournament and dominated everyone. Then in the regional championship game against Wichita State, Rudy Macklin broke his finger. He was our leading scorer and leading rebounder. He was our catalyst all year long. Not having him at full strength took an edge off the Final Four.

And then President Reagan was shot the weekend of the Final Four. One of our players, Mark Alcorn, was dying of cancer. Mark was sitting on our bench. He won the most courageous athlete of the year award. Unbelievable feelings were running through my head. I remember walking out on the floor at the Final Four. That was the year I was named by NBC and *The Sporting News* as the national coach of the year, but none of it seemed to matter. The games, the awards, none of it really mattered. It was so obvious that there were a lot more important things going on in the world.

I had this terrible pain because I knew the pain Macklin

was going through. I knew the pain the team was going through. After they announced the President was almost dead, I knew the pain a lot of people in the country were going through. I don't even know why we played in the Final Four that weekend. I wished they would have put it off after the news. But the games went on and our heads just weren't there and Indiana defeated us and went on to win the national title.

7

Going for the Big-Time Recruits

Our success in the early 1980s took us to places we had never imagined. By that I mean it took us into the living rooms of some of the nation's hottest recruits. Suddenly we weren't competing with Alabama for a good regional player, we were competing against UCLA, UNLV, and Kentucky for players who could singlehandedly turn a program around.

The outrageous stories of all of our recruiting efforts, though, can't compare to what it was like to get involved with our first ever "big-big time" recruit, John Williams.

I thought we had no chance. John was a McDonald's All-American from Los Angeles. Some people even voted him the high school player of the year. Ron Abernathy was my assistant in charge of national recruiting at the time. He found out that John's mother, Marie Matthews, was from Louisiana. It didn't matter to me. I still didn't think we had a chance to get him. Ron was sure we had a chance because John's mother had decided that she wasn't going to stand for any cheating. They were going to do this honorably. Her son wasn't for sale. She wanted him out of the L.A. area before he got shot . . . or worse.

At Ron Abernathy's recommendation, I went out and met John and his mother. I liked him immediately. John was a toucher, he was a hugger, and he seemed very sincere. But I quickly became nervous. There were a lot of people hanging around him on the fringes, each saying they were his representative. Some supposedly were family, some supposedly were UCLA people, some supposedly were with UNLV, some supposedly from Houston, some supposedly from Louisville. I thought the situation was impossible.

I was further convinced that this wasn't ever going to work for us after sitting in John's house one day when the phone rang. His mother answered. She had earlier recounted all the offers other schools had made, some of which were unbelievable. She answered the phone and talked for a second, then put her hand over the receiver and signaled for me to come and hear the conversation. She didn't have an extension phone so I leaned next to her and listened. The guy on the other end told her that she'd have $150,000 in a trust fund if John signed with his school. He said that the money would be put in a local bank: she would get $25,000 when John showed up, and $25,000 when he signed. He laid out a whole payment schedule to her. I was standing there with my jaw open. There was no way, I thought to myself, that we were ever going to get this fine player.

Later a recruiter for another major school came to the house. I was in the kitchen with Marie, and she peeked out the window to see who was knocking at her front door. She told me to stay in the kitchen where I could hear the conversation.

I could hear him explaining to her how the head coach was feeling a lot of pressure about recruiting John due to an ongoing NCAA investigation of their school. The plan was to tell the newspaper that the school was backing away from recruiting John so the heat would be diverted. "But," he told her, "that's just what we're going to *say*. The truth is, the deal's still on." The next morning, the Los Angeles *Times* reported exactly what he had promised—that his school was no longer interested in John Williams.

Following one visit to Los Angeles, I came home and contacted the district attorney in L.A. through Ossie Brown, the district attorney in Baton Rouge. I had been told by John's mother that she had been warned in a telephone conversation that if John went to LSU, his body would be found in the bottom of the L.A. reservoir. I even requested police surveillance of their home for a week. The more I saw, the more disenchanted I became with what was going on.

I began thinking of ways to make the point of how disgusting all this recruiting had gotten to be. I decided to borrow $150,000 from the bank and take it out to Los Angeles in a money belt. I knew exactly how I was going to play this out. Before I did it, though, I thought I had better call LSU's chancellor. I told him, "I'm going to the bank to get a hundred fifty thousand dollars. I'm going out to L.A. and I'm laying it all out on the table in front of John Williams and his mother, and I'm telling them, 'There's a hundred fifty thousand dollars. That matches your highest offer.'" Then I was going to pull another dollar out of my pocket and I was going to say, "Plus here's a dollar, which makes me the highest bidder. Now that I'm the highest bidder, I've got a meat truck out here with cold storage, and we're taking you back to Baton Rouge right now." This whole recruiting game had been reduced to exactly that—being the highest bidder on high-priced meat, and I wanted to let John hear that message loud and clear. The chancellor said, "Oh please, don't do that. What if you got in a plane accident and they found the money on you? What if you were stopped by the police? No one would understand your point." Anyway, after talking to him, I decided not to do it.

Another afternoon Ron came in to my office and said, "John's mom, Marie, has real problems. Her car has broken down and she can't get to work. John has been sick and staying home. He put a plastic bowl in the oven to cook some food and it caught on fire. It burned up the oven. Her landlord said he was going to kick them all out, including John's grandmother who lives with them. They don't have five hundred dollars to their name, and she needs a loan of fifteen thousand dollars. Is there any way we can lead her to someone who can loan it to her? Coach, I don't know what to do, but I hate to lose John. What do you think?"

I looked at Ron and said, "I cannot believe this, Ron. What if this is a game? Let me think about it. I am tired of going after the top recruits and losing them due to situations like this. Let me see if I can get a plan of my own." I went home and decided to talk to my wife about it. Vonnie is Miss Super Straight. She thinks a venial sin is a mortal sin. I said to her, "You won't believe what happened today with John Williams. Ron Abernathy told me that John's mom needs a fifteen thousand dollar loan. She doesn't want the money illegally, she wants a legal loan. She's working, but the bills are mounting. What do you think I ought to do?" Vonnie looked at me real plainly and said, "I'll tell you what I think. I think you should get her the loan. I'm sick and tired of all this cheating. This happens every year, Dale, and we always lose out in the end." Then she turned around and went to bed.

I sat there thinking that was a heck of a fix she left me in. I stayed up until one o'clock in the morning debating with my-

Me as a child in Minot. *Courtesy Dale Brown*

Hang time—Minot State University. *Courtesy Dale Brown*

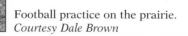

Football practice on the prairie.
Courtesy Dale Brown

My family in 1972, after I took the LSU job (Vonnie, Robyn, and me). *Courtesy LSU Sports Information*

Me and Jack Schalow (my first assistant, now assistant with the Portland Trailblazers) handing out nets across the state in 1972.
Courtesy LSU Sports Information

The love of basketball descends from grandfather to grandson (1992 NCAA tournament, with Christopher). *Courtesy LSU Sports Information*

Two North Dakota boys—Roger Maris and me.
Courtesy LSU Sports Information

Truly a living saint—Mother Teresa, Calcutta, 1993.
Courtesy LSU Sports Information

The wizard (John Wooden)
and the Baron (Adolph Rupp)
at an honor banquet at LSU.
*Courtesy LSU Sports
Information*

The thrill of victory sure beats the agony of defeat. 1986 NCAA
Regional Final. *Courtesy LSU Sports Information*

Dick Vitale telling me "You need another TO, baby!" I guess he didn't know the game was over.
Courtesy LSU Sports Information

My pal Bobby Cremins and I before we do battle again in the NCAA Regional Final.
Courtesy LSU Sports Information

Longtime friends—Eddie Sutton and I visit before tip off.
Courtesy LSU Sports Information

Chris Jackson (Mahmoud Abdul-Rauf), one of the all-time great players and an even better human being.
Courtesy Dale Brown

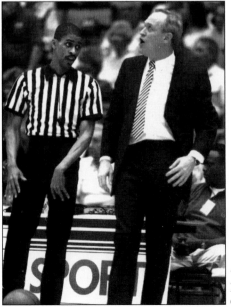

Vonnie, me, and five-month-old Christopher—a pre-game surprise at my 400th career win.
Courtesy LSU Sports Information

"It was on the floor, Coach." "Are you kidding? He was tackled in midair!"
Courtesy LSU Sports Information

Another Shaq Attack dunk.
Courtesy LSU Sports Information

Clowning around at LSU.
Courtesy LSU Sports Information

At Angola Penitentiary.
Courtesy LSU Sports Information

Moments like these will always be special in a coach's life. *Courtesy LSU Sports Information*

Screen down and post up solid. *Courtesy LSU Sports Information*

You can do it, you just gotta believe! *Courtesy LSU Sports Information*

Goosestepping in a Russian
general's uniform, a gift from
Dr. Alexander Gomelski, former
Russian Olympic coach.
Courtesy LSU Sports Information

The best potential of "me" is "we." *Courtesy LSU Sports Information*

self and finally decided to try to do it legally. I would go to a bank and have the proper papers drawn up for Marie. She had a former husband who lived in Louisiana. I would get him to sign the papers and it would all be legal. So at one A.M. I went to bed. At four o'clock, I was still lying there with my eyes wide open wondering if this is legal. It was certainly very close to the thin line. Too close for comfort. Finally, I said to myself, "Nope, I am not doing it." I was able to go to sleep.

When I got to the office the next morning, I called Ron Abernathy in to talk. "Ron, I've made a decision," I said. "I'm not going to do it." He just straightened out his arms and looked really mad. "Ron, I know how you feel. You have worked so hard, but I just can't do it." "Oh no," he said. "Coach, I'm so glad you made that decision. I feel the same way." Together we called Marie and explained the whole situation. She understood completely.

When Marie asked us to help her get a loan for $15,000, I could think of a hundred reasons why it would have been an honorable thing to do. But it would have been a first step in the wrong direction. It would have been a little erosion. The next step—really cheating—would have been easier to do. I respected Marie a great deal because our decision never caused her to waver.

Once we had gone through all of this, my head was telling me that we should just back off. There was no way we were going to win, no way we were going to get into a bidding war with these other people. However, Ron said we had to give it just one more shot. Ron and I took a 6:00 A.M. flight to California. We spent the entire day in California with John, then flew to Memphis, where we hopped on a private plane and flew to Marianna, Arkansas, to sign a player, then back to Baton Rouge.

By the time we got back to Baton Rouge, it was four in the

morning. We stopped by our office to pick up Ron's car and to check my messages. There was a note on my desk from our basketball secretary telling me to call her as soon as I got in. So I called her at home at 4:00 A.M. She said, "Marie Matthews has been trying to get in touch with you. It's an emergency, and you must call her back immediately." So I called Marie at four in the morning. I explained to her where we had been. She said, "You have to come back out here right now. Something has happened."

What had happened was that John had been taken to the house of a big, well-known college basketball booster and was separated from his mother. They apparently made him a great offer. She said, "You just have to come out here right now. I'm not going to let anybody buy him off." I told Ron to go home and take a shower; we were going to catch the 6:00 A.M. flight back to California. I went home and showered, drove to the airport, and got back on the same plane to L.A. that we had taken the previous day. We met Marie at a hotel and by that time she had found John. He was very cold to me at first. He wasn't the John that I remembered. Marie was very insistent. "John, you have to make a decision. *You* have to do this." Before we arrived in L.A., I'd explained to Ron that I would only stay one hour. After that, I was getting my coat and leaving, and would not recruit him any further. Ron agreed.

I must have given John a fifty-minute speech on why he should come to LSU, then sat there another ten minutes. Ron Abernathy was sitting on a little credenza and John was sitting on the couch. Finally, I looked at my watch and said, "Well, John, I'm really disappointed." I got up to get my coat. "Whatever you do . . ." In the middle of my sentence, Ron jumped in and said, "John, when are we gonna quit being niggers?" John looked at him with his eyes wide open and said, "Give me the pen." He took the pen and he signed to play at LSU. His mother was sitting next to him in a chair. She jumped up, hugged Ron, and she cried, "God, you saved my baby, you saved my baby."

Getting John was a real breakthrough for our program. He was a great kid, too. A perfect example of his class was after we were embarrassed by David Robinson and Navy in the 1985 NCAA tournament. Walking down the hall on the way to a press conference, he put his arm around me and he said, "Coach, I really feel sorry for you. You told us what was happening and we weren't smart enough to wake up to it. I can tell you one thing. Next year, I'm leading you to the Final Four."

The next year, I was downstairs before our second game in the NCAA tournament against Memphis State. There sat John with his hand all swollen and the doctors all huddled around him. I asked what the heck had happened. Every time they touched it, John was wincing and screaming in pain. Apparently John had had diarrhea so one of the student trainers sent him to the student infirmary. They were feeding him intravenously and the needle broke off. All the glucose was stuck in his hand.

The doctor looked at me and said, "I don't know if he can play." That's just great, I thought. We were playing Memphis State. They were number three in the nation. The doctor said he'd try to give him a shot to reduce the swelling and maybe it would help. I went out to the court, and there came John. He played four games over the next two weeks. He was catching the ball with his left hand and bringing it in to his right hand. Despite everything the doctors did, they could not get the swelling down. He couldn't even bend his wrist back and shoot the ball correctly. Yet, as predicted, he led us all the way to the Final Four in Dallas. He really did play with pain. We lost in Dallas, but we were in the Finals because John was willing to do whatever it took to get us there.

After that trip to the Final Four, John decided to turn professional. We talked about it. He cried. He didn't want to leave. I asked him about his reasons for leaving. He kept saying, "I gotta, Coach. I gotta." But he never explained it. Losing John was a real blow. There are stars and superstars. There are so very few players that ever become superstars. The superstars, in my opinion, are the guys who make everyone else around them better. Julius Erving was a superstar, Magic Johnson was a superstar, Larry Bird was a superstar, Bill Walton was a superstar. Michael Jordan was not a superstar early. He was a star, but found out, and he admits it, that the Bulls couldn't win until he became a superstar who lifted others as well.

John Williams truly was a superstar. He had all the talent in the world. Of all the stars that I've coached, he had the most tremendous ability to lift others, on the court and off the court. It is sad to me to see him struggle in the NBA, but I believe there are several reasons for that. He was nineteen years old when he left LSU. I also think there were too many parasites hanging on him—he was one of the most sensitive young people I've ever met in my life and he just wasn't ready to deal with them.

Having gone through the John Williams experience I began thinking about not recruiting the stars anymore. No more top recruits. There are so few times that these situations do not occur. Although none of this happened when we recruited Shaquille O'Neal, it seems like with a great number of top recruits, everyone expects something. If their "uncles" don't expect something, somebody else in their family does, or they do themselves. There is a primadonna attitude that has developed, a feeling of "you owe it to us." You've got to call a hundred times. You've got to come to all-star games. You've got to hang around the halls at their high schools. Most of these superstars profess that they are bothered by all the attention. That's really simple to solve: sign early if you're bothered. But there just seems to be so much extra baggage with superstars.

I believe recruiting is actually cleaner now than it has been in the past. I think there are fewer reasons to cheat because there is more flexibility in the rules. Dick Schultz, who ran the NCAA for five years and was a man I really respected, had a lot to do with that. I think the NCAA has begun to penalize people, not just schools, and I think that's important. I think people—the players, the boosters and the coaches—who are involved in cheating are suffering the consequences. That has been a big help and I feel the new NCAA executive director, Cedric Dempsey, will pick up where Dick left off.

8

Gestapo Bastards

When you start winning on the court and recruiting well off of it—especially at a school not known as a basketball power—one phrase starts being whispered about you in the world of college sports: they must be cheating. It is like being one of the richest men in the world and wining and dining a woman, who then decides to marry some poor guy. You probably could not accept that maybe she just didn't love you. You would probably say the poor guy gave her drugs or something. You have got to make excuses for being turned down. That's exactly what happens in college sports. If you offer a kid $150,000 and he goes someplace else, you immediately say the other guy bought the kid for more. For those people who have offered big money, it is hard to believe that others could have done it the right way. There is no profession with more jealousy. Everyone badmouths everyone else in recruiting.

Gestapo Bastards

Obviously, by getting John Williams, there were a few folks out there saying those things about us. Given that, combined with my constant criticism of the rules and the governing body of college sports, the NCAA, I should not have been surprised that they might try to shut me up by investigating us. The investigation, which lasted four years and was one of the longest ever in NCAA history, was the most degrading experience of my life. I thought it was a witch hunt. I believed it was because I was vociferous, because I stood up when others would not.

It all started in 1975 with the publication of a book called *Athletes for Sale*, written by two Washington *Post* reporters whom I respect very much, Leonard Shapiro and Ken Denlinger. I was barely getting the program off the ground, and had three losing seasons. But I guess they knew that I had a big mouth, so they thought I would talk to them. Most people don't talk and I talk too much. I said some pretty powerful things in the book.

But it was a statement I made in the book that was central to my trouble. Leonard asked me what would I change about college sports and I said very simply, "I would change the NCAA. They legislate against human dignity. And the executive director, Walter Byers, is an isolated guy that no one knows. It definitely has to be revolutionized."

After the book was published I called the NCAA headquarters for a rule interpretation, and Warren Brown answered the phone. He was the assistant to Byers. I was ready to hang up the phone when Warren said, "Dale, are you going to be in the office this afternoon? Walter Byers wants to talk to you." "About what?" I asked. "About some of the comments you made about the NCAA in that book." It was obvious that Byers was trying to intimidate me from speaking out, and I got mad instantly. "Oh, is that right? Well, you tell Walter Byers that

91
●

the initials of this country are USA, they are not USSR," and I hung up.

Several years later, as I continued my quest to make a difference, I tried to work with the NCAA. I wanted to meet with Walter Byers at his office in Kansas City. I wanted to clear the air, to get it all out on the table, and to get everyone to just tell the truth about college athletics. I thought it best to bring my attorney and to tape record it all. Of course, Byers never talked to me. David Berst, the NCAA's head of enforcement, called me back and said, "Mr. Byers has made a decision. You can come, but there will be no recording of the meeting and you will have to come alone." I said, "Hold on. I'm not gonna buy that. I can't record it and I can't have an attorney. I'm not coming." I think it turned them off because they knew then how little I trusted them.

I wanted to appeal to them to reach out and change college athletics, yet here they were, closing the door in my face. I wanted to work within the system, but no one would listen. So, in my typical fashion, I figured out a way to get them to listen. I talked about them every time I could in speeches and press conferences. I felt I was right. I was wrong. In retrospect, the whole thing was a mistake on my part. There are so many other things I could have been doing that were more worthwhile.

It probably didn't help that I called their investigators "Gestapo bastards" in a magazine article. But the largest part of my problem has always been that the NCAA has a whole bunch of rules that actually make it harder for those of us who are trying to do it honorably. Experiences like mine cause the good guys not to want to stand up to the NCAA. They don't want to go through what I did. And the bad guys are certainly not going to say anything. If you're a murderer, you can hardly complain about the rules against double parking. Well, the

Gestapo Bastards

NCAA is too worried about double parking and jaywalking when they should be cracking down on murder and assault.

In 1982, the NCAA came after me. They looked under every rock, and through every trash can. They spent all their time interviewing players that left, or players that I asked to leave the team because they had problems. And despite all that work, the NCAA came up with—in four and a half years—eight pieces of lint, none of which involved any one on our coaching staff.

The eight minor violations the NCAA finally charged us with were:

1. During the fall of 1983–84 academic year Dr. Jack Andonie, a representative of the university's athletic interests, purchased four sets of complimentary season basketball tickets from student-athlete Theron Cojoe for approximately $500.

Jack Andonie was the president of the Board of Supervisors, one of the top doctors in the South, and one of the finest Christian men in the whole world.

Players used to be able to sell their tickets. Then the rule changed. All of our players were then told that they could not sell tickets. But one day, one of our managers walked into Theron Cojoe's room and he heard him say, "Okay, Dr. Jack, I'll be sure and do it. I'll send you the tickets." The manager reported it to me. He said, "Coach, I don't know what that meant." But I thought I knew. So I called Theron Cojoe into my office. I said, "Theron, I've got a question. Did you sell your tickets to Dr. Andonie?" "Absolutely not," he said. "I did not do that at all, I swear." I said, "You're sure you didn't?" He nodded his head.

I dialed Dr. Andonie's number. At that time I didn't really know him that well, but I was blunt. "Doc, can I ask you a question? Did you buy Theron Cojoe's tickets?" "Sure I did," he said. "Doc," I said, "are you aware the rule changed last year? You can't buy a player's tickets." He said, "You've got to be fooling. No one told me." I said, "Doc, did you send him the money for the tickets?" He told me he would have to check with his secretary to see if the check had already been sent. But he promised not to use the tickets and he said he would mail them back to me.

The bottom line is that Theron Cojoe, a seldom used player, did try to sell him the tickets, but I stopped him. Nevertheless, the NCAA determined that it was a violation. Now, how in the heck could it be a violation? I did what I could to stop it.

2. On occasions during the summers of 1981 and 1983, Al Guglielmo, a representative of the university's athletic interests, permitted members of the team to reside at the Cedar Wood Apartments at no cost to them.

What happened is that one of our players, Steffond John-son, was living with someone who was not on our team. Near the end of the school year when we went around to find out who needed apartments, most of the players raised their hands. If they needed an apartment, Al Guglielmo had the name of an apartment complex that they could afford on their summer job money. Steffond didn't raise his hand, so we didn't help him find an apartment. About halfway through the summer, Steffond and his friend split up. Now he had no place to live, so he went to one of the apartments that our guys were renting and asked if he could throw a mattress on the floor and stay there the rest of the summer. As part of their scholar-ship, the apartment was already paid for by the other two players. So Steffond stayed there the rest of the summer sleeping on the floor on a mattress.

The NCAA, therefore, claimed that Mr. Guglielmo gave players free rent. We showed them all the documentation you could ask for to prove that the guys who rented the apartment had paid for it. But the NCAA said Steffond received free rent. Whose fault is it if he didn't pay rent to his teammates? Is it my fault? Is it Al Guglielmo's fault?

3. During December of 1982 Al Guglielmo lent Steffond Johnson a hundred dollars to enable the young man to drive from the university to his home in Longview, Texas.

There was an incident where Steffond broke our training rules and I made a decision that Steffond needed to go play elsewhere. The next day he came to the office and I said, "I don't want to play games with the media, but I will do this: if you quit by six o'clock today and explain that you are going to transfer, then you'll beat me to the announcement that I will make tomorrow that you are not coming back." So he quit, saying he wanted more playing time. No one from the press asked me if he was suspended from the team, so I never had to reply. I simply said I wished him the best.

As he was getting ready to leave, he came by my office and told me he was first going back to his home before heading to his new school. He came with tears in his eyes, saying that he loved LSU and thanking me for everything we had done. He said, "Coach, is there any way you can loan me a hundred dollars? I have four tires that are so bald I can see the air through them. I'm never going to get home." I told him I couldn't help. He said, "Is there any way you can get one of the alumni to borrow me the money?" Again, I said no. Finally, I'd had enough. I said, "Steffond, I've given you all that I can to help you succeed, and here you are asking to borrow a hundred dollars. Now, I'll tell you what I'll do because I feel sorry for you. If you want to stay in Baton Rouge an extra couple of days, I'll call Mr. Guglielmo and see if you can get a maintenance job at his apartments."

Steffond was very grateful, so I called Al. But Al said he wanted no part in helping Steffond out. I said, "Al, let's not kick the guy in the head while he's down. How about letting him come over and work for a few days. Would you do that for me?" Al agreed, so I sent Steffond over.

As soon as Steffond got there, he started in. "Al, I have a problem. I don't have any gas in my car and these tires are not even gonna make it to work. Could I get the advance of the hundred dollars I'm gonna make, and then I'll work it off?" I don't think Al wanted to have to keep up with all this, so he just agreed to get Steffond out of the office. Bad judgment.

Steffond took the hundred dollars and never showed up for work. He went back to Longview, Texas. Now, here is a guy that is not even on our team. He's going to another school. That was one of our eight pieces of lint. How ridiculous.

4. *During the fall of 1982–83, student-athlete Theron Cojoe sold two complimentary basketball tickets for four home games to Al Guglielmo for a hundred and fifty dollars.*

Al Guglielmo had the best seats in the house. His season tickets were the best. So Theron Cojoe tried to sell him seats? Give me a break.

Theron said Al bought his seats. Al said he didn't. The NCAA never interviewed Al to ask his opinion. They just took the word of Theron Cojoe, whom they interviewed after he left the team.

5. *During the fall of 1982, a medical doctor, who was a representative of the university's athletic interests, provided*

medical consultation and arranged for treatment for an enrolled
student-athlete at no cost.

Take one guess who that was—Steffond Johnson. Steffond came to me while he was working here during the summer before his freshman year. He had not even played a basketball game. He said, "Coach, you will not believe what has happened. My mother she thinks she's got cancer of the breast. She's got a great big lump in there. Is there anything that you can possibly do to help? She's got no insurance. Coach, if she dies this is the last person I've got on this earth."

I felt terrible. I said, "Steffond, I can't get anybody to help her, especially an LSU doctor. That is against the rules. I'll tell you what I'll do. I'll call a doctor and find out if he knows anyone she can see." I called a friend of mine who is a doctor in town and I told him I didn't want anybody associated with LSU to get involved. He had someone he thought could help. This doctor he recommended was an Ole Miss graduate, and didn't have anything to do with LSU. I told my friend that Steffond's mom didn't have any insurance and it would be great if he could just set up some kind of billing plan.

Steffond called his mother, who took a bus over here from Texas. The doctor discovered that she did have breast cancer, but he was able to remove it safely. The tumor was malignant. They billed her for eleven solid months, telling her to pay just $25 a month, $50 a month, whatever she could. Now, if I had to do it again, I would do exactly the same thing. If that was a violation, I'll accept it.

6. During the 1982 and 1983 academic years, Tom Moran, a
representative of the university's athletic interests, entertained
several of the university's enrolled and prospective student-

athletes in men's basketball for meals at Ruth's Chris Steak-house at no cost to them.

That's partially correct. Tom Moran did that. When the players came in, he occasionally did that. No recruit ever got a free meal from Mr. Moran. I told him not to, but he did anyway. I'll admit that was a violation. Trying to be nice is a violation.

7. *During the summer of 1983, Al Guglielmo, a representative of the university's athletic interests, assisted prospective student-athlete Tom Curry in the purchase on credit of a 1982 blue Fairmont automobile from Richard's Ford dealership in Baton Rouge, Louisiana.*

Tom Curry worked for Al. Tom Curry wanted to go look for an automobile. Richard's Ford had some deal in the paper where they were selling repossessed cars. He called Mr. Guglielmo and asked if he would give him a ride out there to look at the car. Al gave him a ride. That is all he did. That is all Tom Curry said happened. That's all Al Guglielmo said happened. Yet the NCAA said Al assisted Tom in the purchase and credit of the car. It is an absolute, one hundred percent lie.

8. *In October 1984 a representative of the university's athletic interest entertained the brother and sister of basketball prospect Tito Horford in the Dominican Republic. Six to eight prospective student athletes were present at this event.*

This one really ate at me. We were recruiting Tito, who was the best basketball player the Dominican Republic had. Carlos Morales, the vice president of the Dominican Republic, invited me to a party on the grounds of a resort called Casa de Campo. While we were sitting at the party, in walked Tito Horford's brother, Tony Baltizar. He walked over to the table and Carlos Morales introduced him. Carlos told me that Tony was his caddie. I said hello, and that was it. Tito's sister was not at the party.

That's it. Those are the eight violations. It is actually a pretty good report card. Now, take all eight and think about the hundreds and hundreds of thousands of dollars that were spent on this business that came up with nothing. I still can't believe it.

I tried to make the whole thing a lot less expensive. When the NCAA investigators came to campus, I told them that I would allow them to strap me up to a lie detector and ask me any question they wished. I promised that if that machine's needle moved one inch toward indicating I wasn't telling the truth, I'd resign my position immediately. They would not take me up on it, saying they did not allow such things. That is another part of the problem. The investigation takes so long that it is like a slow death.

Having gone through the whole mess, I can't imagine anyone else enduring it. This is a system that is so out of control that it can even eat its own, even good people like former NCAA executive director Dick Schultz. What it says to me is that when men try to repress other men, they will set up all kinds of hypocritical rules. When the system gets as foul as this one did it's frightening. Things like this should not happen in the greatest country in the history of the world, the United States of America.

Here was Dick Schultz, one of the great gentlemen in college sports, who winds up losing his job due to this system. The NCAA accused him of knowing about some loans made to student-athletes when he was at Virginia. This is the problem. Just because he was athletic director, he can't possibly know everything. It is the same way for coaches.

We still have to make some significant changes in this organization. But before you get started on reform, you have to agree that most people in this profession are pretty decent guys. There is no question that no matter what kind of economy there is, or what kind of education we have, there will always be high-priced call girls. Some people will always be for sale. That will never change. This is not Utopia. Cheaters are never going to vanish no matter what. But we have a system now that is built on the opposite premise, that most people in the profession are pretty rotten. I happen to believe that is just not true.

It's funny, but until this experience I always felt that if you were judged guilty, then you must be guilty. This experience changed my opinions about a lot of things. TV analyst Al McGuire said, "Dale Brown is trying to create changes in the NCAA to help athletes and is so vulnerable, they'll reopen Devil's Island if he's done anything wrong."

I still think the NCAA owes my family and me a public apology for what they did. It was wrong and I believe they know it was wrong. It meant a lot to me when one of the NCAA staff members came to me after we had faced the infractions committee and said, "Dale, I want to say something to you. I personally feel that we owe you an apology. What happened here was a disgrace."

A couple of years later, Doug left the NCAA and went to work for the University of Miami, which is the school Tito Horford transferred to. I invited him to come visit with me the day of an LSU/Miami football game in Baton Rouge. Doug accepted the invitation and came by the office before the game. We buried the hatchet, and we did so that day. We occasionally even talk to one another these days.

What I told the authors of *Athletes for Sale* years ago about how we must change the system is still true. But I'm no longer going to be the torchbearer for change. It is too much work.

Gestapo Bastards

You lose too much; you lose your concentration. My whole life has been spent whipping the system. I don't want to joust with the windmills anymore. I need to go in other directions. Let some other young turk handle that. Unfortunately, no one has stepped up.

9

Wrestling Naked

I wasted a lot of time during the last decade doing something I really regret: feuding with Bob Knight. I should never have let the situation get to the point it did, but I'm glad to say that it is all behind us.

The first time we played against Bob was in 1981. We were in the Final Four and were playing them in Philadelphia. When one of the referees was running down the court, Bob stood up and said, "Get those guys off our back." The referee never said anything to Bob. The referee came down to my end so I stood up and said, "Why don't you sit him down," pointing to Knight. He looked at me and said, "You sit down or you're going to get a technical." That told me this wasn't going to be a fair situation. The referee wouldn't say anything to Knight, but didn't hesitate to threaten me; I even ended up with a technical foul.

I just chalked that one up to experience. But in 1987, we played Indiana again. This one was for the right to go to the Final Four. We were twelve points ahead and the situation repeated itself. It all fell apart because everyone was afraid of Bob Knight. First, he got a technical foul for going out on the floor. Then he came over to former Notre Dame athletic director Gene Corrigan, who was at the official scorer's table as a representative of the NCAA, and said, "You've got to do something about these blind bastards," pointing to the referees. Then he took his fist and pounded the phone sitting on the scorer's table so hard that the phone receiver popped up in the air. I looked at the NCAA people. They just sat there with their arms crossed.

I said to myself, "If I would have done that I would have been banned from the game. There would have been headline stories." Then Bob actually grabbed one of the referees by the arm before our player shot a technical foul. He kicked his bench, and the only reason the benches didn't fall over was because they were all attached to each other.

From that point on, those officials bellied up to Coach Knight. The rest of the calls in the game were in his favor. I went back and watched the film. Sure enough, all but a couple of the next seventeen calls went for Indiana. On one play toward the end of the game, one of their players grabbed our ballhandler and got a lot of body and a little ball. The referees called a jump ball. The ball went to Indiana. On another play, one of our guys got hit four different times while he was dribbling the ball near halfcourt. They called him for five seconds. Coach Knight was later fined $10,000 by the NCAA, but Indiana went on to win the national championship in our home away from home—the Superdome.

I had a quick decision to make and my thought was not to shake the man's hand after the game, but just go on to the press conference. Then I realized I would be a poor loser. They beat us and I knew there would be a time and a place where we would get it back. I went on and shook his hand. I knew, however, that I had to do something about this. I went to the press conference and did not say anything about his tirade.

When I got on the team bus my daughter, Robyn, was there. She was very emotional. I said, "What's wrong, Robyn? We lost a game, big deal. We'll be back." She said, "That doesn't have anything to do with it, Daddy. What Coach Knight did, that was wrong. Especially for that old man." That sent a red flag up to me. I said, "What did he do?"

She explained it very thoroughly. She said, "I know he probably didn't recognize me, but when he came through the tunnel, he stopped and looked up into the crowd. With a diabolic look on his face he said, 'Hey, you LSU people. I stuck it to you again.' Then he turned to run into the dressing room. As he did there was an old man on the other side of the walkway. I don't even know if he was an LSU fan. The old man yelled to Coach Knight that he didn't think Coach Knight should talk like that, especially after winning the game. Coach Knight turned back and yelled an obscenity at him, too."

I took off out of the bus and headed for the Indiana dressing room. By the time I got down there, they were gone. I ran down the hallway just in time to see their bus drive off. As I headed back to our bus, Hank Nichols, the head of officials at that time, was coming out of a room. I called him aside and I said, "Hank, enough is enough. That conduct out there was ridiculous. You're the head of officials and you let him get away with that. Somebody's got to stop this man." Hank looked at me and shuffled his feet. "Well, Dale," he said. I interrupted him, "Don't give me that. It's the way you guys all start your sentences—'Well, Dale.' He's wrong and you know he's wrong." Hank said, "I'll admit he's wrong." So I asked,

"Why don't you say something about it, Hank?" He just walked away.

I went back and got on our bus, determined that I was going to face Bob with this. The next week at the Final Four in New Orleans, Bob Costas had me on his radio show and he said, "We understand you don't have a lot of respect for Bob Knight." I felt sure he was setting me up. I just said "Yeah." And Costas said, "Well, Bob Knight made a statement about you, too. He said that when Indiana was twelve points down, and it seemed as if he might lose the game, he looked over at the bench and saw Dale Brown was coaching. He wasn't worried anymore."

I said, "The way to settle this would be to put me and Coach Knight in a wrestling room naked and whoever came out first would be the best man. I'm sick of him bullying and kicking people around."

That made its way around pretty quickly. Then it got to be a name-calling deal. He would say smart things about how he was not worried about LSU or Dale Brown. I would say something back. It was like two kids, and both of us resisted attempts by mutual friends like Pete Newell and C.M. Newton to get us together.

A year later, I was at the Final Four talking to Coach Bob Boyd. He was sitting at a table in a hotel restaurant and I was down on one knee beside the table. Over to one side were several of Knight's former assistants, Dave Bliss, Bob Weltich and Don DeVoe. All of a sudden, I spot Knight. Man, my ears got red. I figured he was going to come over and talk to his assistants, so I would have a little confrontation with him. I was staring at him as he got near, but he wouldn't look at me. Knight walked by and he hit Bob Boyd on the back, but he did not say anything to me. I stuck my leg out as far as I could, hoping he would trip over it. I figured I would just deck him and get it out of my system. I looked like that old cartoon figure, the Plastic Man, with my leg stretched out as far as I could get it. Somehow he stepped over my leg and nothing happened.

Shortly after I hired Tex Winter, who is now an assistant with the Chicago Bulls, he told me a story. Tex said that one year he had tried to nominate me for the National Association of Basketball Coaches board of directors. Bob Knight was on the board of the NABC. He had mentioned to Knight that I would be a good choice for the position on the board. Bob said to Tex, "I don't want that cheatin' son of a bitch on this board." I got really mad. What he was saying was that we had to cheat to win, but Indiana doesn't have to. I had that in my craw for a long time.

Just as my disdain for him was really getting to be too much, a twenty-eight-year-old girl was killed in Baton Rouge. She was driving home and somebody threw a brick through her windshield and killed her. I was reading the story in the paper, and thinking about how painful it must be to lose your daughter like that. If that happened to our daughter, Robyn, I would probably become a vigilante.

A few days after the incident, a follow-up article was in the Baton Rouge newspaper. The police had found the killers. The newspaper interviewed the girl's father, a doctor by the name of James Upp. His wife had died of cancer prior to this happening, now his daughter was dead too. In the interview, the reporter asked Dr. Upp what he thought when he saw the picture of the young boys on television. Dr. Upp said, "Well, they certainly look like clean-cut youngsters and I have no malice or anger toward them. I am sure they did not mean to kill my daughter, and I forgive them. I only wish they could have met my beautiful daughter. I think they could have learned from her."

I read that story, and it just took everything out of me. I thought to myself that I wanted to live my life as Dr. Upp wrote. I cut the article out and I was going to put it up on the bulletin board in my office. As I started to do so, I realized I was being counterfeit. I sat there knowing how much I disliked Coach Knight. I could not put that on my bulletin board as long as I had all that anger for him. That father could forgive those boys for taking his daughter's life, and I could not even forgive someone for something so trivial as our conflict. I put the clipping down on my desk and I opened the coaches directory. I looked up Indiana University, and I dialed the number. The secretary answered the phone and I said, "Bob Knight, please." She asked who was calling and I replied, "Dale Brown." I could hear her swallow hard on the other end.

Bob picked up the line. I started, "Bob, you can hang up anytime you want to but I want to tell you something. I want to tell you about an incident that happened here in Baton Rouge." I told him all about the girl, and then what Dr. Upp had said. Then I explained to him, "I was getting ready to put this clipping on my bulletin board, but I knew I couldn't because of my contempt for you. I'm going to tell you right now, if I'm gonna put this clipping up, I want to bury the hatchet with you. I want to forgive you. And if I did something to ask for any of your actions, I want to apologize."

Suddenly, it was as though the whole slate was clean. He said, "Dale, I'm sorry." He apologized for the incident that had upset Robyn. He said, "I appreciate your call and I want to bury the hatchet. Maybe we can work on a friendship." From that day on it was as if a cross was lifted off my back because I'm not a hateful person.

A year later, I tried to reach out again, calling Indiana and offering Bob's son a scholarship to LSU after Bob suspended him from the team.

Tiger in a Lion's Den

Calling him was one of the hardest things I have ever done. First of all, I didn't know what I would receive from the other end. And I wasn't humble enough to do that naturally. I'm sorry that it took a death to teach me that lesson. But anger and hatred only weigh you down and kill a part of you. By hating, you are really losing twice.

10

For Those Outside the Arena

All I would ever ask of anyone in the media is to be honest, fair and report positive accomplishments more often. Unfortunately, that is not always how it is done. Aside from college sports, the media has done much in the last twenty years to hurt America by its negativism, sensationalism, and cynicism. There just does not seem to be anything good going on in this country if you judge by reading the front page.

I really became aware of that in 1981. I do not usually join organizations, but there is one called Dreams Come True that I like. It is a nonprofit organization that grants terminally ill children their last wishes. A man called me and told me about a little nine-year-old boy dying of brain cancer. His last wishes were to go to Disney World and to get an autographed basketball from LSU. He wanted to know if I could bring a ball out that Sunday afternoon. I got an autographed basketball, and I drove to the little boy's home. I opened the door and there was one of our players, Johnny Jones. He was a freshman who is now one of my assistant coaches. He was holding the little boy.

I thought to myself, "This story will lift a lot of people." So I called the radio stations, the television stations, and the newspapers. I told them Johnny was there and that I thought it would be a beautiful story. No one showed up. However, had Johnny Jones been arrested for drunken driving on the way back to the athletic dorm, *Eyewitness News* would have been there for a live shot and every reporter would have been there with their pad. It hit me right then that not enough attention is paid to the good things that are going on in this world.

A reporter came into the dressing room after our loss in the NCAA tournament and asked, "This is several years in a row you haven't taken your team out of the first round of the NCAA tournament. I know the people of Louisiana are going to be disappointed in you. How do you feel about that?" Well, the first thing I wanted to do was choke him. Instead, I said, "Before I answer that question, let me ask you a question. Do you ever have anything that uplifts anyone? Why didn't you come in and ask if I was gratified that this was the tenth NCAA tournament in a row that LSU had been to? Why didn't you ask if I was gratified that only two other schools, Duke and North Carolina, had a longer streak?" He looked at me and said, "Is that the truth?" He did not even know.

My problems with some in the press probably spring from the fact I'm not fearful of them. I think some of them resent the fact that I will not cater to them. I always downplay my role as head coach, instead pointing out what a good job the assistants did. That usually gets me eliminated from most lists of "genius coaches." You know what's funny about that? We ran an offense while I was at Minot State that is as good as any offense in the college basketball world. There are only so many things you can do with five people on a court measuring 94′ by 50′. This is a very simple game. Dean Smith is a great coach at a great basketball school, but calling his four corners offense a stroke of genius was a little much. Think about it. There are only four corners on the court. Where the heck else are you going to go?

I have learned that those in the media who are telling the world how good or bad you are sometimes have no clue what they are talking about. A few years ago, we played a small school named Houston Baptist. They held the ball the whole time and we won 62–60. When I got home that night I turned on the television to watch scores from other games. The sportscaster came on and said, "LSU played a very poor team tonight, but Dale Brown had better work on his offense. First of all, there's not enough motion in that offense. The ball isn't being moved around enough and as a result they only scored 62 points."

At the time, I had a radio show at Ruth's Chris Steakhouse. During the show that next week, in walks this sportscaster. After the show, I called him over and said, "How would you rate yourself compared to the other sports announcers in this town?" He said, "I think I'm one of the best." I told him I agreed. Then I asked him to grab a napkin and just draw me a diagram of how we set up our offense. He did not have any idea what I was alluding to. He looked at me for an instant, then said he really did not pay much attention to it but he would try. He started scribbling. I asked him, "What are those X's for?" He said, "I'm just trying to set up your offense." I told him that X's are never offense, X's are always used to mark the defense. He started drawing again and then asked for my help. I showed him how we ran out of what is called a double stack with a point guard. I drew it for him, then asked him to show me one option out of that offense. He said, "Well, I don't really know how you start it." To make a long story short, after about ten minutes of this routine, he got the picture. I asked him how in the heck he could go on television the previous week and say there should be more motion in our offense when he did not know what he was talking about.

That is how reputations are built, and often they are built incorrectly. When one of them reports, "Dale Brown can recruit and motivate, but he can't coach," it becomes easier for the next guy to say it. Before you know it, that's what everyone believes is true. And that is my reputation in some circles. When I hear it, I just laugh. Without sounding egotistical, I sometimes ask the critics: How can you get to a Final Four with a six-foot-six guard playing center if you can't coach? How can you win the second greatest number of games in the history of the SEC if you can't coach? How can there be only ten coaches in the history of this game who have been to more NCAA tournaments than I have if I can't coach? How can the guy who took the lowest seed ever to the Final Four not be able to coach? How can the only coach to beat the first, second and third seeds in an NCAA Regional not be able to coach?

The problem is that no one challenges the press when they criticize. Coaches with poor records do not challenge them. Coaches who want to stroke them do not challenge them. A percentage of sportswriters seem to take great joy in building you up and then trying to chop you down. I did not get into coaching for the cheers or the jeers.

I keep a copy of a short article in my wallet. It's a clipping out of a New York paper that was written after Indiana beat us a couple of years ago. It reads, "Again Dale Brown proved he cannot coach." I've kept that clipping so that when we do win the national championship, I will pull it out and with graciousness say, "To all you people who are underdogs and don't think you're any good, and who had people knocking you down, I want to read something to you. We have just won the national championship, which I'm real happy about, but this is what a writer said. He may even be here now." Then I'll remind the media of what I have said over and over again. Players win the games, coaches do not.

When it comes to the media, I have to admit I am sometimes my own worst enemy. A good example of that came early in my career at LSU when we were playing Kentucky. The week prior to the game, John Wooden had an article in *Sports Illustrated*. In it he said he did not like what was happening to the game of basketball. He believed it had become brutal. The game should not be, he said, a full contact, knock 'em down, scrape 'em up off the floor, type of sport. I agreed with him.

We went to play Kentucky, and they were a very good team. They had Rick Robey, James Lee, and Mike Phillips. Big bruisers. They beat us pretty good and after the game Billy Reed, a writer who was with the Louisville *Courier-Journal*, asked me what I thought of Kentucky's style. I said, "When you get waxed like we did, you must have a great deal of respect for the program. But just as John Wooden said last week, I do not respect that physical style. They brutalize the game with their strength." Well, he gets mad at me and he just did not like my answer.

He came right back at me. "Do you mean to tell me your team is simon pure and doesn't do anything wrong?" I thought, "If you think you are going to intimidate me just because I got my butt kicked by thirty points in Lexington, you have another think coming." All sorts of thoughts were running through my mind before I actually answered the question. I just blurted out, "The only way I can answer a stupid question like you just asked, is to ask one just as stupid. Have you ever masturbated in your life?"

His story the next day cut me to pieces. And since that day, he needles me every chance he gets. Writers are supposed to be fair. But too often a great number of them are very opinionated. They carry hatred with them. I do not dislike Billy Reed, but I do not expect that he has much use for me.

The other problem is that media people in general want to please each other. And the only way to do that is to rip into somebody. I never really understood that until a local reporter wrote a very nice article about me in the Baton Rouge paper. The next time I saw him I said, "I want to thank you. That was very humbling. It was really a nice article." He looked at me and said, "Boy, did I catch hell for that article. Everyone at the paper accused me of kissing Dale Brown's butt. Anytime you write a positive article, other writers are all over your case." What a lousy way to live.

I don't want it to sound like I feel this way about all of the folks I have met in the media. There are some really genuine and beautiful guys in the business too. But those guys are not selfish and jealous, nor are they hero worshipers.

The media's influence on fans is somewhat frightening. And I'll tell you, some of the fans I've seen in my twenty-two years in the SEC didn't need any influencing. Kenny Higgs, who was one of our first ever really talented recruits, had epilepsy. Kenny was from Kentucky, but had decided to come play for LSU. During his freshman year, we were playing in Kentucky. Just before the game started, this man who looked to be about forty years old came by our bench. He yelled, "HIGGS!" Kenny glanced over at him. I turned around about the same time. The man glared at Kenny and said, "We'd just as soon have a leper on our team than an epileptic." Then he turned and ran off laughing. That kind of thing just turns your stomach. You start wondering if these people have anything good happening in their lives. The problem is that fans have never been held accountable like the athletes and coaches.

When Chris Jackson (Mahmoud Abdul-Rauf) was at LSU, there was an article that said Chris did not know who his father was. The next week, we went to play at Mississippi State. Fans there chanted, "Where's your father, Chris? Where's your father?" The next year, we went back and a group of students were taunting the team because Shaquille had not come out for early warm-ups. They were yelling, "Where's that big African? Bring out the big African."

In visiting arenas, I have been hit in the back of the head by a hot coin, a coin that had been held by a pair of tweezers and heated. I walked off the court in Tennessee and heard someone hollering my name. As I looked up, the guy spit on me. When I got back to Baton Rouge, I received a letter from the security policeman who was standing next to me. He apologized, even though it was not his fault.

A few years after I took over at LSU, I took my daughter to Gainesville, Florida, for a game. She was fifteen years old. I had her sit on the bench with the team. It was the first and last time she will ever do that. The Florida students taunted me, "Dale, who's the little broad you have with you on your bench." I was walking off of the court at halftime the next day, concentrating on what I would say to the team, and all of a sudden I heard someone next to me say, "I'm going to kill you, Brown." I looked up and there was a guy glaring at me, full of anger. I grabbed him and two security policemen stepped in. I smacked him up against the wall and said, "Arrest this guy." The next thing I knew my arms were pulled behind my back and the security guard was pulling me out of there. I said, "What the heck are you doing?" The security officer explained that the guy was a photographer. The guy swore he did not say he was going to kill me, but instead said that our team was getting killed. If he was with the media, he should not have said that either. Some of the media cut me apart the next day, saying I was out of control.

We could all learn from the University of Arkansas. I have never been so impressed with fans as I have with the University of Arkansas. We have lost up there two years in a row. But the fans were great. They did not come by and rub it in. They were pure class. After one of their games in Baton Rouge, I joked that they stole the ball from us so often I was going to call 911 for being mugged. The next week, an Arkansas fan sent me a portable telephone to bring with me to Fayetteville. When we got up there, we all stood up for the pregame introductions, and the fans held up signs that said DALE CALL 911. It was really cute.

We had the honor (chuckle) of losing to Arkansas in the last game ever played in their old Barnhill Arena. I was leaving the arena to get on the bus after the game, and I stopped there for a moment to watch the ceremony to say goodbye to the arena. They brought back many of their old players and coaches for the event. I decided to tell the fans there how great it had been to compete against them. I asked Frank Broyles, their athletic director, if I could speak. I said, "I want you to know how much I respect the way you all operate as fans. You have fun. You're clean. It's fun to come up here. Of course, I've got to be your most popular guy since I've never won up here." You can't believe the nice letters I received from their fans.

Sometimes I have been disappointed with some of our own fans. I have heard them yell at me not to "put that foreigner" in a game. I heard them yell at some of our players, booing them even before they ran down the court once. Those things really bother me. When you pay the price of admission,

116

●

what liberties does it allow you? Does it give you the right to boo and hiss when somebody is trying hard? There is so much pain in the world—cancer, death, unemployment, divorce, bankruptcy. Why would these people want to come to a game and not enjoy it? Why go to a game if you can't enjoy the beauty of it, if you can't enjoy the imperfection? Does it make people feel good to boo or hurt someone else?

I believe John Wooden said it best when it comes to fans and the media: "As a coach, you'll receive a huge amount of unjustifiable criticism and a large amount of undeserved praise, and you should not be unduly affected by either."

The ultimate combination of fanatical fans and out-of-control media types is on display during the explosion of radio call-in shows. Rick Pitino had a great analysis of call-in shows. He figured a majority of the folks who call in are the unemployed with nothing better to do than share their negativism. There are not many call-in shows that are ever of a complimentary or constructive nature.

Most hosts of call-in shows appear to use their show as a release or a way of becoming the coach. And most of the callers are just venomous and vindictive; they're mean. They feel they have the right to say anything about anyone. I would make a bet, although I can't prove this, that 90 percent of people who call in do not have a season ticket, are not backers and have been to a few games. It's too bad Sirhan Sirhan, Lee Harvey Oswald, John Wilkes Booth, and James Earl Ray weren't basketball fans who participated in call-in shows. If they would have taken all their venom out on the coaches and players, they might not have assassinated people. There is truly a bizarre mentality that exists in our country—praise people, then cut them down.

When those of us who are cut up during these shows start complaining, they hide behind the First Amendment. I just want to know where there is a First Amendment for those of us in the public eye. Where do we have protection? I'm not free from sin and mistakes, but why should I have to be cut open in front of the world because I'm a basketball coach? It is the same thing that has happened with criminals. Criminals have more rights in this country than the victim has anymore.

Author Kurt Luedtke once said that the media has lost sight of the fact that "other people have rights, too." He's correct in far too many instances. The real pros in the media have class, and I respect them immensely. They aren't house boys or cynics. Thanks to all of you in the media who have not succumbed to the temptation of a quick fix, but continue to be honest. I admire you.

11

Discovering Shaquille

I have always enjoyed foreign travel and I've been fortunate enough to do quite a bit of it. I have especially enjoyed some of the basketball clinics I have taught while on those trips. Many of the experiences I've had on those visits abroad have changed my life. But few can compare to what happened when I was teaching a clinic at a military base on the East German border, at Wildflecken, West Germany. I was there on behalf of the United States Army, and had been speaking up and down the East German border. I would speak to officers on leadership and enlisted men on teamwork. I agreed to do one basketball skills clinic. I had just finished my lecture during the basketball clinic when this hulk of a man came over to me. He had to be 6'7" and had filled out pretty well. He had good-looking shoulders and huge feet.

"Coach, could you recommend some exercises for my

legs," he asked. He told me that as big as he was, he could not dunk. He admitted that he did not have any real basketball skills. I demonstrated a couple of exercises. Then I looked at his feet and asked, "How long have you been in the service?" He looked at me and said, "Coach, I'm only thirteen years old."

I'm no dummy. "Is your father around?" I asked. He told me his dad was in the sauna. "Please, take me to him," I said. We walked over to where his father was getting out of the sauna. I introduced myself, handed my card to him and said "Sergeant, I'm Dale Brown, the basketball coach at LSU. I had a nice visit with your son. I think he can develop into a player, and I want to keep in touch."

Sgt. Philip Harrison is a big man. He held his hand up for me to stop. "I don't mean to be rude," he said, "but I'm very concerned with blacks starting to develop some intellectual-ism so that they can be presidents of corporations instead of janitors, head coaches instead of assistants, and generals in-stead of sergeants like myself. If you are interested in my son's educational and intellectual capabilities, we might talk some-day."

I stuck my hand out and I said, "Sergeant, you and I are going to be good friends. I love the philosophy you have. I agree with you one hundred percent."

I started corresponding with their family, keeping up with Shaquille, even though the next year he was cut from his high school team. I had an address for them in Germany, and I had an address for a grandmother in New Jersey. I came home and told our coaching staff this kid was going to be seven feet tall and have a really big body.

I never saw Shaquille play until he came to the United States. When his father transferred to San Antonio, my assist-ant, Craig Carse, and I went over to watch his summer league game. The only other college coach there was from some small school. It was obvious that Shaquille was raw. He could run and could block shots, but the game was not yet part of him. But you could also tell he had a great attitude.

At that game I realized another important point: his mother had as good an attitude as his father had shown. She sat very quietly during the game. She just sat and enjoyed the game. She was not hollering at the referees. She wasn't like those parents who live their children's lives.

As a senior at Cole High School, Shaquille led his team to a state championship. He had really developed into a player and everyone around the country started showing up to recruit him. Fortunately, Shaquille didn't forget that we had been there from the beginning. He came for a campus visit and was a perfect gentlemen.

It was probably the most clean and honorable, simplistic recruiting effort I have ever dealt with. Everything was aboveboard, everything was strict and everything was disciplined. There was no attempt to drag it out and get more publicity. Shaquille signed early. I really thought this family should be the beacon light for everyone with a son being recruited because he was a highly sought after player whose recruiting was never questioned. In all of my recruiting of high profile players, never have I ever met a family that was less complicated, or more determined to do things exactly by the rules.

And that continued with Shaquille even after he came to LSU. Never have I had an athlete come to me and ask more questions about what the NCAA rules were and weren't. For example, we were playing in the U.S. Olympic Festival in Minneapolis. After a game one night, Shaquille came to me and said, "Coach, I want to introduce you to this man. He's a school principal up here and played with my father in high school. He wants me to come to his house tonight and eat. Can I do that? That's not against an NCAA rule is it?" Neither Shaquille nor his family ever asked for any special favors.

I really became fond of Philip and Lucille Harrison. Lucille is a special woman. Philip would call me for advice. Anytime our LSU cheerleaders would go to San Antonio for a contest, he would invite them all to the house and have a barbecue. Whenever I'd go to San Antonio, he refused to let me get a rental car or taxi. He always greeted me with great big bear hugs. It was just the greatest relationship.

Things changed some as Shaquille's career took off at LSU. Philip became more involved, more opinionated and more critical. I am much the same way, so I understood him.

That was a part of the one aspect of Shaquille's career at LSU that I wished had turned out differently, and it began to disrupt our efforts to teach him some different scoring moves. He was not one hundred percent interested in shooting the hook or the turnaround jumper. He knew he was so big and powerful that he could dunk almost all the time. But I said, "Shaquille, this isn't gonna work. You're gonna get double-teamed, you're gonna get triple-teamed in this league." In an effort to make him better, I arranged for two of the greatest players to ever play the game, Bill Walton and Kareem Abdul Jabbar, to come in and tutor him. (The NCAA, in its great wisdom, has now eliminated this teaching tool.)

I asked Bill to come down for four days to work with Shaquille. He was absolutely brilliant. He worked on post-up moves and passing. Then I got in touch with Kareem. I told him that I wanted him to teach Shaquille the hook. Even with both of those all-stars teaching Shaquille, I noticed that he was barely interested.

Not long after that, I received a call from Philip. I never talk to parents about players' skills. If you start taking those calls, you'll go goofy. Right off the bat, Philip spoke up, "Coach, can I ask you a question? Why did you bring in Jabbar and Walton to work with Shaquille?" I was surprised by the question. "First of all, Jabbar has the greatest hook ever in the history of the game and he is one of the greatest players who ever played the game; second, Walton probably had better knowledge of the inside/outside game, finding people and kicking the ball out, than any other player in the history of the game. I want to make sure, as we work to develop Shaquille, that I don't leave any stone unturned."

There was a little pause. Then he said, "Coach, I would prefer Shaquille use his power and dunk everything he can." I thought about it for second, then said, "Philip, you said I was to be Shaquille's father away from home as well as his coach. You've given me that leeway, and I think that has worked well for Shaquille's best. Let's leave it that way." He got the message and never questioned me again.

After all that, Shaquille did make some great improvements. But he always seemed to resort back to his old habits of ducking his head and dunking the ball.

I felt bad that during Shaquille's career at LSU, he got caught up in some of the dirty politics of Louisiana. It happened after an interview during which Shaquille was asked if he would have chosen LSU had David Duke, the founder of the National Association for Advancement of White People, been governor. Shaquille said, "I came to Louisiana because of Coach Brown, his assistant coaches, and the program. I didn't come because of the governor."

Well, David Duke took that comment and used it during a national interview of his own. He told the interviewer that Shaquille's comments proved that people who said his election would hurt Louisiana were wrong. Duke said, "Well, Shaquille O'Neal, the great all-American, said he would have come to Louisiana regardless if I'm governor or not."

That's not really what Shaquille said and David Duke

knew it. But he was using Shaquille for his own good. Shaquille asked to have a press conference and set the record straight. I was proud of him for doing this.

Unfortunately, one of the raps that is laid on Shaquille—and me, too—is that we didn't get to the Final Four with Chris Jackson (Mahmoud Abdul-Rauf), Stanley Roberts, and Shaquille O'Neal on the team. It is very simple. Chris was a sophomore, Stanley and Shaquille were freshmen. That group played together only one year. Had they stuck together, I could better understand the criticism. Michigan State did not win it during Magic Johnson's first year. And they had good talent all around him. David Robinson never won a championship, Olajuwon never won a championship, Mutombo and Mourning never won the title and they played together. The whole rap is so preposterous.

During his sophomore and junior years, we did not have a true point guard. When Chris went early to the NBA, we were not able to recruit a solid backup. And in college basketball, you are in serious trouble without a point guard. The college game is not a big man's game anymore. One of the reasons is that officials do not know how to referee with big guys. I thought Shaquille took the worst shaft his first two years in the SEC. He would block a shot, the other guy would fall on the floor, and the ref would call a foul on Shaquille. Referees in our league would say, "Shut up and don't be a crybaby. Look how big and strong you are." His size has nothing to do with whether he is being fouled or not. As long as they were not going to call the game properly, it would continue to hurt his game even more.

I loved working with Shaquille. He was an inspiration. He was fun to have around. But he was right to make the decision to turn pro after his junior year. He had accomplished all that he could in college and, as he quickly proved, he was ready for the NBA. His initiation into the NBA has been outstanding and he's getting better all the time. He deserves all of it.

Before the start of Shaquille's second season in the NBA, *Sport Magazine* asked me to write a letter to Shaquille to be published in their magazine. I wrote the letter. The magazine writer called me back and said, "I talked to my editor and he wants to know if you could possibly say something about his poor free-throw shooting and other problems." I replied, "Wait a minute, you guys asked me to write this article, didn't you? Either take it the way I wrote it or just don't print it." He called back again and said, "Could you change just a few things?" I told him. "Now, if you guys want to write something, then write it. But don't try to put words in my mouth."

They never ran my letter. But in it I wrote, "Shaquille, you must now be very conscientious. You are on top now and there are going to be many people coming after you—from groupies to agents to relatives. You have to be very careful of parasites. I hope you never lose that contagious smile that you have. It will be hard not to get the big head. Also, don't be conscious of criticism that is unfounded. Sometimes people will say things about you because you are a big man. If you don't win it all or get into the playoffs, some people will call you a failure. You will be considered a loser because you have a big body. They are wrong, Shaquille. You are not a failure and you will never be a loser. The thing I will remember most about you is the way you treated my wife, my daughter, and grandchild. You know what matters in life. If you ever need me, I am here to help you."

I am sorry they never printed that letter. He is a very special person. One of the most impressive things about him is that he is exactly what he says he is. When he says he does not do drugs, he doesn't. When he says he doesn't drink, he doesn't. When he says he's going to get his education, rest assured he'll graduate from LSU. In fact, he came back to summer school at LSU in 1994.

And it is a real accomplishment when you overcome the temptations that present themselves to a young and famous millionaire. I have always said that I was not impressed by someone's claim of chastity if they work in a bank in Harvey, North Dakota, a town of 2,500. But I am impressed if you are an international businessman and you have been to Paris, Rome, and Algiers and have resisted those temptations. The same thing applies to Shaquille.

All of these honors that have been bestowed upon Shaquille will make these next few years the biggest challenge of his life. But I do not think he is going to change. I think he has too much good in him.

The summer before his second season in the NBA, I worked with Shaquille at a Reebok clinic in Japan. We met at the airport and took off for the arena. Ten thousand people were there waiting. The people supervising the event told me I was supposed to sit out on the court, while Shaquille was to make a grand entrance. They had a giant screen with all kinds of psychedelic colors and music. All of a sudden, the announcer boomed out, "And now, ladies and gentlemen, please look at the screen." It showed Shaquille coming out of the dressing room with a towel slung around his neck and a scowl all over his face. The crowd was ooh-ing and ahh-ing as Shaquille was stalking down the hall with a bodyguard.

I was watching all this on the screen. Shaquille came out and walked to the stage. He grabbed the microphone and said a few words in Japanese, still wearing that scowl. Then they introduced me.

I took the microphone and asked two of our former players who were in the audience to join Shaquille and me. Dennis Tracey, who was a walk-on guard, and Vernel Singleton, one of our greatest hustlers, who was playing professionally in Japan, came down. I told the crowd, "The message I would like to leave with all of you is that while we are all here today hailing Shaquille O'Neal, he got where he is today because of his teammates. Here is a walk-on who passed him the ball. Next to him is a guy no one in college basketball wanted, but he became a fine major college player. The lesson is that while not all of us can be Shaquille O'Neal, we might be Dennis Tracey or Vernel Singleton. And that's important, too."

There were many little Japanese boys and girls encircling the court, the cutest little things. So when I finished my speech I went over to Shaquille and asked, "Shaquille, what was that junk that just happened back there? You looked like Mr. Mean coming on stage. That's not Shaquille O'Neal." He said, "Coach, they told me to do it." I said, "Shaquille, that's just not you. Be the Shaquille that all of us loved. See all those little children, go over and tap them on the head and pick them up and shake their hands."

I left the floor and started heading up to meet my daughter in the stands. When I got there, Robyn told me to turn around and look. There was Shaquille picking up little kids and hugging them. The next day, the story in the *Japan Times* was about the gentle giant, Shaquille O'Neal. Shaquille needs to be Shaquille. That, as I learned very early on, will make him one of the finest people in sports.

12

Sap, with a Capital S

My wife, Vonnie, likes to joke that I collect stray people the same way that some people collect stray cats. Sometimes I get burned when I try to help these people, making me feel like I have SAP stamped across my forehead, and a bright light from a miner's cap pointed down on it.

There are dozens of examples, dating all the way back to my earliest days in the business. While I was coaching at Garfield Junior High in Berkeley, California, I was introduced to a youngster from a rough neighborhood, and I felt he had the potential to really make something of himself. As a result, I got him a scholarship to go on to college, expecting great things from him.

I tried to stay in touch with him. After I took the job at LSU, I invited him to our game every time we played on the

West Coast. I tried to help him here and there, but never anything big.

Then suddenly he disappeared for a while. In November 1986, I got a letter from him, saying that he had completed a drug program and had been living on the street. He asked that I help him out again.

I said to myself, "Boy, oh boy, you are your brother's keeper. I should reach out and help, even though he had lied to me on a couple of occasions. We all make mistakes."

I called our athletic director and told him about this guy who had been on drugs and was living on the streets. I explained that I would like to get him off of the street, get him cleaned up and dressed up nicely, and then bring him to Baton Rouge to talk to the team. We could give him an honorarium. I would call around the state to other universities to see if they could help him with speaking engagements. He was bright, articulate, and could talk about the evils of drugs. The athletic director agreed to do it. We decided to pay him $500 to come and speak, plus another $500 for his airplane fare back and forth.

Due to the fact that he needed help immediately, I personally paid for his airfare, thinking he could give it back to me after the university paid him.

He came to Baton Rouge and we got him all dressed up. I took him to my home and bought him a suit and some other things he needed. He looked really nice, and he spoke to the team. It was a very inspiring speech. By then, I had gotten another speech lined up for him as well. So I sat down with him and offered to help him formulate a brochure for a speaker's bureau. "I really admire what you are doing," I said. "Talking about your situation is the first step toward controlling it. I want to help you as much as I possibly can to get your life in order."

The university check was given to him just prior to his departure, and the banks were closed. So I told him to cash the check when he got back to California and send me the $500 for airfare.

Not only did I never receive my $500, but I have never gotten anything from him. Not a letter, not a thank you—nothing. I felt really used—like a Sap.

A really outrageous story involves a fellow named Mozar Cezar. His nickname was Gato, which means "cat" in Spanish; a name that would later prove to be ironic. Gato was from Brazil. One day I received a letter from him asking me if he could come to Baton Rouge and study under me. He wanted to learn basketball. Although I had never met him before, I decided to bring him to LSU. He became part of our basketball family and my wife included him in our family functions. We bought him clothes and helped him financially, plus let him travel with our team on road trips. He sat in on our staff meetings and came to practice everyday. He was a quiet and very nice man. For one full year he was part of us.

At the end of the year, he confided in me, "Coach, I'm learning so much. I want to be the greatest coach in my country. I want to stay another year, but I ran out of money. I've sold my refrigerator, my television, even my car to pay for this last year. Can you help me get a job?" We had a job available as a dorm proctor living in the basketball section, so I gave it to him. It didn't pay much, but it helped him. He continued to live in the dorm and I paid him some extra money out of my own pocket. After all, he was part of our family.

Halfway through the basketball season a friend of mine, the national coach in Lebanon, escaped an assassination attempt. He made it to Cyprus, then out of the country. He was seeking political asylum. He wrote to the United States officials, "My name is Henry Yabrudi. I'm a Lebanese citizen applying for political asylum in the United States. I was a member of the Lebanese Falagis [Phalange] party, which belongs to a major group generally known as the Christian Force, but is also known as the Lebanese Force. Two of the dominant figures of the Lebanese Force were Ellegal Beeki and Samar Jakar. We fell out of favor with Jakar. My brother was detained and beaten. Now they are after me."

Henry got in touch with me and asked if I could help him obtain a green card. I set up a meeting for him with Lawrence Fabacher, a very sharp immigration attorney in New Orleans. To make a long story short, Henry got his green card and moved to California.

Well, sometime earlier, Mozar had asked me to help him obtain a green card so he could stay in the United States legally. I explained to him that he could not get one because he was not seeking political asylum. After Henry got his green card, Gato could not understand why he couldn't get a green card if another basketball coach could get one. He could not grasp the concept that Henry was from Lebanon and was a man in danger within his own country, where Gato had no such problem in Brazil.

A week later, I was in the shower with twenty minutes to spare before my evening speech at Stetson University in Deland, Florida. Just as I stepped out, the phone rang. It was Craig Carse, one of my assistants. "Coach," he said slowly, "sit down. Something has happened." "Oh no," I panicked, still dripping wet. "Is it Robyn?" "No," he answered. "But you're not going to believe this. Gato has climbed into the tiger cage. He swears he has a bomb in a bag and he is going to kill Mike the Tiger unless he can get a green card. He's holding up a sign that says 'Dale Brown is unfair.'" "Craig, are you joking?" I said. "Coach, I swear I'm not kidding. I feel so sorry for him, some of the crowd is hollering 'Feed him to the tiger, feed him to the tiger,' you know, making fun of the guy. Your wife and daughter are here, and so is the SWAT team. They said they will have to shoot him if he goes for the bag. They think he's crazy, and he is yelling out your name." I dashed downstairs and tried to keep my mind on the speech I was delivering. It wasn't easy.

After the speech, I called my wife and daughter. They were panicstricken. Gato had set it up so that he would be on national television for the six o'clock news. The tiger cage, where our LSU mascot, Mike, is kept, sits right next to the basketball arena. So all of the live shots had our arena in the background.

I caught a flight home the next morning. By the time I arrived in Baton Rouge, they had gotten him out of the tiger cage. Jose Vargas, one of our players who spoke Spanish, had talked him out. He was then arrested. I put up a $10,000 bond to get him out of jail, and he was admitted into a mental hospital to be checked out. They assured me he was not crazy. He began crying and apologizing, and I said, "Gato, how can you do this to me?" He just continued crying and telling me he was sorry. I explained to him that he would have to go back to his own country. He cried even more and said he couldn't go back because he owed his wife child support and they would arrest him when he landed if he didn't immediately pay her $2,000.

So here is another example of my being a Sap, with a capital S. I not only bought him an airplane ticket, but I gave him $2,000. I had state trooper Mike O'Neil transport him from this mental facility to New Orleans, where he caught a flight to Rio de Janeiro. When I got back to LSU, I made a statement to the press, "The sad incident of last evening is over. What happened to Gato could have happened to anyone. His personal problems were overwhelming and he simply snapped. We truly are our brother's keeper, and last night this man needed his brothers. The police displayed the highest professional standards and great compassion. Jose Vargas, I'm so proud of you. On the court of life you are a superstar. Your behavior and grace under pressure is what our program is all about. To those who shouted 'tiger bait,' what can I say? May you never experience sadness and loneliness, and may you find the love that you couldn't give."

Now, the truth is, I wanted to strangle him for what he did, frightening my family and the team. As I thought about it, I realized that the poor guy probably couldn't help himself. But I have never heard from Gato again.

I guess when you get burned a few good times like that, most folks would stop putting themselves in such positions. That's just not my style. I never lose my faith in people because I have my own perspective. I think that most people don't plan to take advantage of others. They don't set out to do it. Sure, there are some charlatans who are manipulators; they are cunning and will use and hurt others, but I can never stop trying to help people. I do it because I often think about the people who have helped me along the road of life.

Without one of those people, I would not have my master's degree. While we were still living in North Dakota, I wanted to go to the University of Oregon because they had a top physical education program. I went to the bank and requested a loan to help with tuition. I didn't have any credit, I didn't have any collateral. The bank wouldn't give me the loan.

As I was walking out of the bank, a man by the name of Jim Norton, who worked there, asked what was wrong. I told him that I wanted to go back to school for my master's degree, but the bank would not loan me the money. He strode over to the cashier, drew $300 out of his personal account, and handed it to me. "You pay me back when you can," he said. I worked as hard as I could to pay him back as fast as possible.

That was an awful lot of faith he put in me and I wasn't going to let him down. Unfortunately, as I've learned, some other people just are not like that.

I simply have to be more selective in who I help and who I don't help. I am a Sap. I am not stupid, but I think my heart is bigger than my brain sometimes. I need to take more time and evaluate better, but some things will continue to happen because I don't want to let the first person go that I can help. For each negative experience, I have at least fifty positive ones. That fact alone continues to restore my faith.

One of the most unbelievable situations I have ever been involved in occurred in the Louisiana State prison system. Every four years I try to take the team to Angola State Penitentiary, which is considered extremely rough and tough. This experience involved a man named Ulysses Long, whom I had met when we took our team to the prison twelve years earlier.

As I was driving around the prison with the warden, I asked him how many men he had in that prison. "About forty-seven hundred," he answered. "What are they like?" I asked. "Whew, Dale, some of them are absolute animals—rape, maim, incest, just terrible," he replied. "Well, is there anyone who doesn't belong here?" I asked. He answered that there was one guy who definitely did not belong in prison, Ulysses Long. Apparently, as a young boy Ulysses made a terrible mistake. He and three other boys held up a store one night. The clerk recognized Ulysses and turned him in. Ulysses refused to turn state's evidence against the other boys or identify them in any way, so as a result he was sentenced to thirty years in prison.

"But," explained the warden, "he is different. He is the meanest, toughest son of a gun when it comes to standing up for what is right; he has broken up more homosexual rapes, more drug deals, more murders than I can count. He started a radio station here, becoming the nation's first inmate disc jockey licensed by the FCC for an FM radio station. He's a very spiritual man. The guy is unbelievable." I admitted to the warden that I had known Ulysses for almost twelve years myself. I had met him on one of the team trips to the prison. He had interviewed us on his radio station, and we had named him an honorary coach. I thought that it was worth trying to get him out. The warden agreed.

During the next year, I stood in front of the parole board and pled Ulysses' case along with the warden. The board gave him the parole. Since it still required the governor's signature, I called Governor Edwin Edwards. I explained to him that Ulysses was really a good guy who had made a mistake. If he would sign the parole and give him a chance, I had a place for him to go and would bankroll him with some money to get started.

The governor agreed. Weeks went by. One of my former players, Don Redden, died of a heart attack. I was walking into the church to give the eulogy and the minister approached me. "Coach, you have an emergency call from Governor Edwards." I picked up the phone, and the governor said, "Dale, I hate to bother you, but I started thinking that I really don't know Ulysses. If I sign this parole, how do I know that he will not go out and commit another crime. That would make me feel guilty and make you feel terrible. If you can't give me one good reason to take this chance, I can't sign this parole, Dale."

My first thought was that someone had hit me in the head with a two by four. First in the front of my head, with the death of Don Redden, and now in the back of the head with this news. "Edwin," I replied, "if you sign this and he commits one criminal act, I'll resign my job at LSU. That is how much faith I have in this guy." There was a long pause. Finally, he answered, "I believe you," and hung up.

He signed the parole papers and I drove to Angola and picked Ulysses up from jail. It was one of the most phenomenal days and nights of my life. I had never seen anyone so happy. He stood on the corner and listened to the sounds of the traffic. That night we went out and looked at the moon. He hadn't seen the moon in over twenty years. Even small things had escaped him in all that time. He did not even know how to use the soda machines in the cafeteria, the ones that require you to push on the front to dispense the soda and ice into your cup.

I had been given a brand-new tailored suit by Hart Schaffner & Marx after I spoke at their national convention. I put the suit on him, and it fit him to a T. He attended his final parole hearing and pardon in that suit. He didn't have a winter coat and he was going to live in Minneapolis. I had a big winter coat with fur that was just his size, so I gave it to him. He is quite a speaker, so I helped him get into public speaking. His speech is titled "One mistake can ruin the rest of your life."

I contacted Gordon Olson, the ex-governor of North Dakota, who is an attorney and the president of a bank in Minnesota. I asked him if he could help Ulysses. He did, and they have been friends since.

It is now six years since he has been out of prison. He is living a wonderful life. He sat on the bench at the game for the gold medal at the Olympic Festival, where I was coaching a team led by Shaquille O'Neal.

I have had Ulysses come back to Baton Rouge to speak to our team. He told them, "Isn't it amazing, guys. My three bro's who were with me the night of my crime, not one of them has ever thanked me. They've never written me. They've never come to see me. I never gave the state their names and, as a result, I got a long sentence. The warden said he would let me out in a year if I told him the names of the other guys. But today I'm here because two men gave me my freedom, Gordon Olson and Dale Brown. They're white aren't they? That's why you can't judge people by their skin. In life, not everything is a black and white issue. And let me tell you, don't make one mistake. I made a terrible mistake one night. But I wanted to be one of the boys, one of the bro's. And none of them have ever talked to me. Let that be a lesson in who your friends are." It was a powerful moment.

I take the kids to the prison for several reasons. I want them to see what the other side of the fence is like. I'm curious myself. I also do it hoping that maybe there is someone in that prison who would be touched by our concern. Some of the prisoners are just con artists who only want money and pardons, but there are also the Ulysses Longs who can be helped.

So for all of the experiences where I've been taken advantage of, there is no doubt I'll take them in exchange for helping one man like Ulysses Long.

One of the most phenomenal experiences I've had in the prison system was with Leslie Lowenfield. I had taken the team to see death row and the electric chair. Ron Abernathy came over and said, "Coach, there is a guy over here you have to meet. He is from Guyana and he has an unbelievable story." So I went over to meet him. He told me that he had come to the United States with a dream of becoming a longshoreman. He ended up in New Orleans. He had been found guilty of multiple murders, but he swore he was not guilty.

But, I thought to myself, no one in prison thinks they are guilty. Not Charles Manson, not Richard Speck, not Ted Bundy. Everyone claims they were framed. Anyway, I listened to his story. He wrote me numerous times after I returned to LSU. He never asked for anything, just wrote nice letters.

One afternoon I was sitting in my office and my secretary came in. She had just heard on the radio that Leslie Lowenfield was going to be electrocuted at midnight. It sent a chill up my spine. I thought about him being all alone; his parents and family were in Guyana. How frightful it must be for him to die alone, even if he did kill someone else. So I phoned the warden and asked if I could spend his last few hours with him. The warden consented, so I drove to Angola. He was in a cell near the death chamber called death watch. I had to go through these big gates with lots of guards, and then I came to his cell. He was shocked to see me there. I said, "Leslie, I'm here for you. I know you are lonely. I'm also here for another reason. I'm not here to judge you, but if you did murder someone, then you should now ask God to forgive you. If you don't, and die with that sin you will find eternal damnation."

He was very gentle and nice, and said, "I didn't kill those people. I was set up, and the police know who did it. My attorney was a no-good guy. For several years while I was here, I never even saw him."

All of a sudden, Leslie got this terrible blank stare off into space. I turned around to see what he's looking at, and there is a man standing by the cell door. "Who is that?" I asked. "He's the attorney that was supposed to represent me." Leslie didn't even respond to him. I asked to be let out of the cell and I walked down the hall with the attorney. I said, "Leslie has told me some very interesting information that makes me believe he might not be guilty."

"He is a pathological liar and con artist. There is no way he's not guilty," he replied. I went back into the cell. Leslie went on to tell me he had been raised honorably in the church, his mother was very religious. He would never do something like this. I began thinking that he knew he was going to die, so what reason would he have to lie to me? Then they came in and started preparing him. They shaved his head and ripped his pant legs, then shaved the hair off his legs so the electrodes could be attached. It really was an ugly sight, but I had to stay. A nun arrived with a priest, and it was twenty minutes before midnight. I left the cell to go visit with the warden.

All of a sudden I heard chains clinking and I knew that they were taking him for the electrocution. There were chains on his legs and arms, chains around his neck and behind his back. I stepped out into the hall and Leslie gave me a smile. He walked toward me, and the guards lowered their guns and let him come over. "Thank you for coming, Coach," he said. He went into the room. There was a microphone there. In the next room, the media and a few witnesses were waiting. Leslie said, "I did not commit this murder and you people know it. I forgive you all and I'm going to heaven." I asked myself if he was sincere or just putting on the final act of a big game.

They strapped him into the chair and they zapped him.

Afterwards there was a press conference. The warden announced without any emotion, "Hello, my name is Warden Elmer Butler. At 12:01 A.M. on July 16, 1987, 23,000 volts of electricity were put through Leslie Lowenfield's body. He grabbed the straps of the chair and thrust his head back. Smoke came up from his temples. He was not pronounced dead. We had to then put 25,600 volts through him. At 12:07 A.M. he was pronounced dead." Then the press asked a few questions and everyone had coffee, orange juice, and donuts, and that was it.

They put him in a body bag and he was done. On the drive home I kept thinking how strange it felt to be that close to a life, then that close to a death—almost as if they were touching one another. I'd never been that close to someone living, then ten minutes later he was dead. Was he guilty? Was he not guilty? There was so much emotion.

Tiger in a Lion's Den

Sometimes in my life I've been a Sap, but sometimes I've been fortunate enough to encounter people and have experiences that a boy from the prairie of North Dakota could never have expected.

13

The White Globetrotter

The dream all started on the fire escape outside our apartment in Minot, North Dakota. I dreamed of traveling. I dreamed of mountains and rivers, towns and cities.

Basketball has allowed me to live that dream. I recently sat down and listed all the countries I have visited, everywhere from Canada to Czechoslovakia, from Iraq to Israel, and from Hong Kong to Haiti. The list was fifty-six nations long.

The experiences that I have had while traveling have been far mightier than the Swiss Alps and much more powerful than the Amazon River. They have taught me how much alike we all are and how gentle and peaceful and loving most of the world is. Contrary to my beliefs about certain sections of the world, we all have a lot in common.

All that travel also made me realize how we, as Americans, are terribly ungrateful for what we have. There is no nation close to America in wealth. Our poorest people are wealthy compared to the people of most countries. Now remember, I have been in the ghettos in this country, all of them. From Watts to Bedford-Stuyvesant, from Detroit's ghettos to the Desire Projects in New Orleans. Yet, I have never seen such pain in the world as in Calcutta when I went to visit Mother Teresa in 1993.

There we saw two dead people in the streets. They had just died overnight of starvation. There were people handing me their starving babies, asking for my help. There were parents who would blind *their own* children because they were sending those children into the streets to beg, because they knew handicapped beggars brought home more money. We were told that many of the poor give up their kidneys and livers for cash. They could earn more by giving up a body part than by working. I went to Calcutta to meet Mother Teresa and came home with a much greater appreciation for America.

Mother Teresa was kind, gentle and polite, but when you were with her, you could see there was steel running up her spine. She was tough and disciplined. Everyone around her respected her and didn't want to disappoint her. She had boundless energy for her years.

One of my main missions in going was to ask her if we could do a basketball game to raise her money. She declined because she said people use her name all the time and she never sees any results from those events. It bothered me that people would take advantage of someone like her.

I also wanted to see what gave her the strength to do what she does, a job that you would think impossible. Her answer was very simple: "I can't do it. God does it." She never complained about the futility of her job, knowing that all her effort was only a drop in the bucket of human suffering. When I asked her how she dealt with that futility, she said, "At least I'm trying. I can't worry about the millions I can't reach. I only worry about those I can."

If everyone adopted her attitude and all those drops were added together, imagine how quickly the bucket would overflow.

One of the things all my traveling has helped to do is expand the boundaries of our recruiting. Over the years our teams have occasionally resembled the United Nations General Assembly. We have had players from Australia, the Dominican Republic, Yugoslavia, Ukraine, Argentina, Netherlands, Spain, and Israel. However, we didn't land 7'4" Lithuanian Arvidas Sabonis, who had told a friend he wanted to play at LSU.

In recruiting those foreign athletes, I have found it a great advantage that they come with no strings attached. They are generally outstanding academically as well. Most do not have parasites trying to get you to give them something. I think having foreign athletes on your team also is an education for the American-born players. We all should be exposed to people from different countries, different religions, and different cultures.

Sometimes, though, it can be difficult to have foreign players on the team because of what might be going on back in their homeland. A good example of that is Danny Moscovitz, a guard we had from Israel. Danny was supposed to be interviewed by a group of reporters in 1992 for a story about foreign players. The day he was supposed to be interviewed, the Iranians started to shoot scud missiles into Israel.

Danny came to me and said, "Coach, I don't want to be interviewed because I recently got out of the Israeli air force and now my family had a scud land down the street from them. I just don't want to start any problems." I agreed with him and went to the press conference in his place. I asked all the members of the media to give Danny a break. I said, "I'm making a plea to you all. Danny Moscovitz is scheduled to be interviewed today. But he's not here because he's concerned about endangering his family. He is also concerned about endangering his team. We travel on private charters and the plane sits out there on the tarmac. Someone could put a bomb in it. I am pleading with you all not to even mention that Moscovitz was not here. Please just drop your story."

The next day the Associated Press ran the story. When I called the reporter, he justified it by saying that I did not say my comments were off the record.

Danny Moscovitz was a nervous wreck thinking something was going to happen to the team or something was going to happen to him. Fortunately, nothing came of it, but it was a dark day for journalism.

The stories of how some of our foreign players made it to Baton Rouge can be as intriguing as any novel. Roman Roubtchenko, who came to us in 1992, is a good example. Roman was a seventeen-year old from Ukraine, playing on the Russian junior national team. The team was in New York City at Kennedy Airport preparing to return to Russia, when Roman and a teammate decided it was their last chance to defect. The KGB agent traveling with them had been vigilant, watching them closely for most of the trip through the United States.

While they were at the airport, Roman told his buddy to grab their passports, which were in their coach's bag. Then the two of them just walked right out the front door of the airport.

They walked for miles before they finally got a taxi. They had $100 between them and could only speak about five words of English. They went into the city and looked around with no clue of where they should go. Roman remembered hearing a song on a musical tape that was about Ukrainian immigrants who lived in Brighton Beach.

Anyway, they wandered around and ended up in Brighton Beach. They wanted to go out in the water because they had never gone swimming in the Atlantic. Both these guys stood out, being 6'8". Everyone noticed them out in the water. This old woman came up and started asking questions. They told this woman their story and she practically adopted them. They had planned to sleep under the pier in Brighton Beach, but she wouldn't hear of it. She invited them to come back and stay at her home. Her son was in the army back in Ukraine, and she said she hoped someone was taking care of him.

They stayed in her home for one night, then in a couple of other homes over the next few days. One of the families found Alexander Volcov, who was an NBA player with Atlanta and was also from Ukraine. They called Alexander, who had already heard about them. Alexander helped them get into a prep school in Connecticut to learn English. While they were there, Roman not only learned English, but he became a top-flight student. We recruited him and he developed into both a solid player and a super student. His teammate is also now on a full scholarship at another Division I school. Don't tell me America isn't the land of opportunity.

I could outlive Methuselah and I could never repay basketball for what it has given to me. The greatest gift has not been a particular win or a game highlight, but it has been the opportunity to go through so many doors with so many people.

14

Special Games—
Special People—
Special Efforts

To encapsulate a handful of great games during my coaching tenure at Louisiana State University seems almost unjust. I could have easily written an entire book of chapters about games that stand out, not just to me but our players, our staff, our university and our fans. Many games are given almost folklore attention with the people in Louisiana and are still talked about today as if they were played yesterday. There have been so many memorable games, great players with tremendous efforts, and emotion-packed excitement. Still, there are a few treasures that are embedded deeply in me when I think back to special games.

It's not the games themselves that stand out. Sure, the exhilaration of winning for high stakes is a great feeling, but unless you have coached in these situations you can never truly understand where the real high comes from. You see, what you have to understand is that to be victorious in special games, you need special people and special efforts. When I think back to those kind of games, I rarely can remember the final score. Instead, I can recall a player or a team overcoming an obstacle, some kind of adversity. You actually see a bunch of individuals form a cohesive unit and come together for the good of a common goal. These are the kind of events that are necessary to pull off the "upset" or advance in pressurized tournament action.

There is a saying among coaches that in preparing a team for a game with practice sessions, game plans, scouting strategies, motivational speeches, your work is largely done by tip off. The phrase commonly used is "the cake is already in the oven." Therefore, I guess the most important part about these special games is not just the "sweet taste" of victory but the "actual mixing of the batter."

It didn't take us long to let the people of Louisiana, the Southeastern Conference, and the nation for that matter, to know what they could expect out of LSU basketball. In my first game as head coach of the Bayou Bengals, we started the season with a home opener against third-ranked Memphis State. These Tigers were a great team and well coached by my friend Gene Bartow. I didn't mind opening up with a challenge, but this was ridiculous. Gene would go on to guide Memphis State to the 1973 NCAA tournament, where wins over South Carolina, Kansas State, and Providence would put him in the national championship against his former team UCLA. A record-setting performance by another friend of mine, Bill Walton, would keep Gene's squad from grabbing the crown.

But this was the previous December, and we had just instilled a new system with a young team and were about to battle against a veteran national contender. That LSU team would go on to be nicknamed "The Hustlers." On that December 5, 1972, night, they were born. We had a tenacious and scrappy defense and a fast-breaking offense, and we stunned Memphis State 94–81 to springboard a 14–10 season.

We were led by Eddie Palubinskas, who scored 32 points, and Bill Whittle, who added 19. But corny as it may sound, it was truly a team effort. The fans were outstanding that night, cheering us throughout the entire game. It was the greatest experience a young coach could have in his first outing. It was hard to explain, but I knew we had the potential to build something special at LSU after that game.

Between the Memphis State game of 1972 and a contest with Kentucky in the Pete Maravich Assembly Center on February 11, 1978, there were a lot of exciting games and landmark victories for our young and building program. Yet on that Saturday I felt our program rose another level, and set a standard for future Tiger teams to live by.

The philosophy of our basketball family, "the best potential of me is we," came full circle in front of 14,551 screaming Bayou Bengal fans. At that time, it was a new Maravich Assembly Center single game attendance record and they were all treated to one of the greatest games in the history of LSU basketball.

Kentucky had a powerful team in 1978. They came into that contest ranked number one in the nation and would back up that ranking by capturing their first national championship under Coach Joe Hall. A former Louisiana native and All-American, Rick Robey, led the powerful Wildcats on to the floor. If we thought we might have trouble matching up with them early, we had no idea of the matchup problems to occur later in the game.

In our earlier game at Lexington, it had been a rough and

tumble affair which was extremely physical and at times had gotten a bit out of hand. Evidently, SEC officials Bill Bennett and Burrell Crowell had decided that contact would not be a big part of this game, and they called it close. I mean *close!* They whistled 65 fouls, and 74 free throws were shot. It affected us greatly, as all five starters fouled out. Still, I could look in the eyes of our reinforcements (we don't call them substitutes at LSU) and see that they believed they could win. In fact, after our 95–94 overtime upset of the top-ranked Wildcats, I commented to the press that "a bunch of guys who believed they could win, won."

The game itself was packed with dramatics, but the overtime itself was unforgettable. With 1:40 remaining in the extra period, Jordy Hultberg, now a sports broadcaster in Baton Rouge, drilled a corner jump shot that put us ahead for good at 90–89. Still ahead by one, we had a great defensive stand, forcing up a Truman Claytor jumper which we turned into a fast break opportunity and a dunk by crowd favorite Floyd Bailey. By this time, fans were in the aisles and forcing their way as close to the court as they could possibly get. The fans had been tremendous as well, and many of our players commented upon how the fans had pushed them through the exhaustion.

It would be a year and a little more than a week until the night of our game against Alabama, played on February 22, 1979. It would mark my seventh season at LSU, with a group of young men who would turn in an effort that would end a drought of magnificent proportions.

We entered the game against the Tide winners of seven straight SEC games and owning a conference record of 13–3. We needed just one win to capture the Southeastern Conference Championship. That night we came out and played with a great intensity that had become our trademark. We blitzed Alabama 86–66 to win LSU's first SEC title in a quarter of a century.

The game itself was a blur. The action was fast-paced and the intensity was unreal. I can recall our team all over the court, diving for loose balls, battling and tipping after every rebound and playing in such a determined state that you just knew sitting on the sideline that there was no way this group of competitors was going to lose on this night. I can still see Al Green capping off the victory with a great dunk and ending a long spell of frustration for the Tigers' faithful.

That Alabama victory sparked the first of three consecutive SEC titles for us, and would culminate in 1981 with a game against Wichita State in the Superdome in New Orleans. It was an NCAA regional final, so the stakes were high with a Final Four berth involved. Playing in front of some rabid home fans and with a team that had previously won 26 straight games and an SEC-best 17 consecutive conference games, we opened up an early lead on the Shockers and built on it before coasting in with a 96–85 win.

The victory sent us to the Final Four for the first time since 1953. We would later be eliminated by eventual national champion Indiana. Going back to the historic win against Wichita State, it is ironic that the one play that stands out in my mind is not a great play or even a positive play. I can still see clearly an inbounds situation with some minor contact between our All-American Rudy Macklin and the Shockers' standout Antoine Carr. The result was a dislocated finger and three stitches for Rudy. Indiana had a great team that year, but I honestly feel that the injury to Rudy was extremely critical in hurting our chances for winning the national championship. I admire the fact that he was so determined to play, but he wasn't at full strength or we would have recorded our twenty-seventh straight victory.

Our next legitimate shot at the Final Four would come again in 1986 against a very familiar opponent and in very familiar circumstances. We had started out the 1985–86 season with a bang, reeling off 14 straight wins. During the regular season, we had two great games against rival Kentucky, losing at the Maravich Assembly Center on a last-second shot and then having the Wildcats pull away late and defeating us in Lexington 68–57. Following the regular season, we found ourselves again in Lexington playing for the SEC tournament. We captured a 72–66 victory over Florida before matching up again with Kentucky. In a devastating case of déjà vu, we again lost in heartbreaking fashion on a last-second shot.

It's kind of strange sometimes how your mind works, but I had the most unbelievable feeling that we would cross paths again with Kentucky before the season was over. I shared this with our team. I vowed that next time would be different.

We started our NCAA tournament run that year in the friendly confines of Baton Rouge but against some unfriendly powerhouse foes. We were definitely in what I thought the most difficult region, and we opened up with a great win over Gene Keady's seventh-ranked Purdue Boilermakers 94–87. Our reward was a contest against twelfth-ranked Memphis State. In a scramble for a loose ball, Anthony Wilson picked up the ball and heaved a miracle desperation jumper that fell and catapulted us to a 83–81 victory. From there it was off to Atlanta to play hometown favorite and sixth-ranked Georgia Tech. Bobby Cremins had put together a strong squad, but Don Redden with 27 and Derrick Taylor with 23 combined for 50 of our team's total 70 points as we defeated the Rambling Wreck 70–64.

The only team that stood in the way of a trip to Dallas and the Final Four was—you guessed it—Kentucky. The Wildcats rolled into the Omni ranked third in the nation and already with three victories over us. Both teams played magnificently, but a balanced attack of John Williams (16 points), Don Redden (15 points), Ricky Blanton (12 points), and Anthony Wilson (12 points) enabled us to pull off the upset in another barn-burning contest, 59–57.

The 1988 season was loaded with heartache as two LSU basketball stars, Pete Maravich and Don Redden, died two months apart with heart failure.

All of us were in shock with the sudden loss of Don, who had helped carry us to the 1986 Final Four. The day before we were to play Vanderbilt in the SEC tournament, we attended Don's funeral, which was especially difficult for the captain of our team, Ricky Blanton, who was Don's best friend. It also took a tremendous toll on me because Don was like a son to me, and I loved him deeply.

The greatest victory I have ever been associated with occurred on March 11, 1988, as a gallant and sorrowful group of young men defeated Vanderbilt 87–80. The game was played for Don Redden, and his best buddy Ricky Blanton once again showed what he was made of as he led us in scoring with 30 points.

New Orleans has been our home away from home, whether we have played in the Lakefront Arena or at the New Orleans Superdome. This past year, our highlight was an upset of third-ranked Oklahoma State at Lakefront Arena. All in all, we are 20–3 in the Crescent City, but none could have been more exciting than our victory over Georgetown, played January 28, 1989.

Georgetown had come into the game ranked number two, but was primed to move into the top spot after the number one team had been beaten earlier. We had been hit hard with injuries and some prop-48 casualties, and the Hoyas were so strong that year that CBS, who had rights to cover the game, had called us and gave us the offer of dropping the game since it was such a mismatch. This only made us more determined to play.

The David and Goliath billing brought fans to the game in record-setting proportions. The paid attendance was 64,144, and 54,321 turned out to make it the largest crowd to ever attend a regular season college basketball game. That record still stands today.

We played Georgetown close early, but they started to pull away midway through the second half before we put together a late flurry to tie the game at 80–80. In one sense, I was amazed at the players who were on the floor when the game ended. Dennis Tracy was a walkon from the New Orleans area who made the team because of an emotional letter he had written to me about his dream to be a Tiger. Russell Grant was another walkon from Louisville who was put in the position to take the shot to try to upset the Hoyas. Ricky Blanton was a spirited player, but was only 6'6" and asked to play center. Chris Jackson was a freshman who was on his way to setting the NCAA record for scoring in a freshman season. Wayne Sims was the cousin of my assistant Johnny Jones and a player who had made the most of his abilities. Still, on the last play of the game, Chris was the object of a Georgetown trap and made a solid play by passing the ball out of the trap to a seemingly open Russell, who took a shot from the right wing only to have it tipped by a rushing Alonzo Mourning. In a mad rush for the loose ball, Wayne tipped the ball to Ricky, who put it in at the buzzer for the upset victory.

I mentioned earlier that in one sense it was amazing to me that these players were on the floor when we finished against

Georgetown. Yet in another sense, this is what LSU basketball has come to mean. Chris Jackson (now Mahmoud Abdul-Rauf) was indeed a great player with tremendous skills, but natural ability on the team ended there. Ricky Blanton has always been one of my favorites for what he has and continues to stand for. He is a self-starter who sets high expectations for himself and has a manlike work ethic to accomplish what he sets out to do, as proven against Georgetown. Dennis now works for Shaquille, and Russell teams with Ricky to run a summer camp in Baton Rouge, which shows that LSU basketball truly does have some family qualities.

Two of the most memorable wins we have had at LSU came within a week in 1990 when we entertained UNLV on January 28 and Loyola Marymount on February 3. Looking back, the caliber of personnel that stepped onto the court that week seems incredible to me. It may have been one of the most talent-laden weeks in the history of the Pete Maravich Assembly Center.

Our 107–105 victory over UNLV, ranked fifth at the time, marked a victory for us over a team that would end up claiming the national championship that year, which concluded with a 103–73 dismantling of a solid Duke team. My friend of many years Jerry Tarkanian had all the pieces in place with a roster that included Larry Johnson, Stacy Augmon, Greg Anthony, Anderson Hunt, and Moses Scurry.

With the game being played as the preliminary to the Super Bowl, Chris Jackson put on a super show by tallying 35 points with shots raining in from all over. Maurice Williamson added another 26 points, and Shaquille O'Neal and Stanley Roberts held their own against the vaunted inside attack of the Rebels. We played solid the entire game and actually built up a 58–49 lead, then held off a furious comeback attack late by Vegas. The Rebels would not only not lose again that year, but would not lose again until they were upset by Duke in the semifinals of the NCAA tournament the following year.

Still, there was no time to rest as twentieth-ranked Loyola Marymount blew into town with more NBA-like talent and an ability to run up points at a record-setting pace behind the newly flaunted fast break attack of Coach Paul Westhead.

In what could be the greatest game ever played in the Maravich Assembly Center, we scored a 148–141 overtime thriller over the Lions. The action got so fast-paced Debbi Polito's play-by-play typewriter actually blew up during the course of the game. I mean they actually did a story on Debbi and her typewriter the next day in the newspaper, where she described the pace as being too much for her IBM. It was almost too much for me. This game was certainly not for the faint of heart.

Loyola Marymount was led by Bo Kimble and by the late Hank Gathers. Gathers, who would tragically die late that season, set a Center record of 48 points, despite having Shaquille block a number of his shots. I can still see Gathers competing in my mind. He was such a tremendous competitor. We should all learn from his example.

The game also marked a performance from Shaq that will be long remembered. How about these numbers for a freshman center: The "Real Deal" scored 20 points, hauled down 24 rebounds and swatted away 12 shots for his first collegiate triple-double. He wasn't alone in the effort. Chris Jackson scored 34 points, Vernel Singleton added 22, and Wayne Sims chipped in 19. But if there was ever a team effort, this was it. We had to play everyone because of the tempo. One of our players, Randy Deval, had trouble coming off the floor at one time because he was so winded. All in all it was a tremendous week of basketball for LSU.

In talking about great games there is something I want to

add, although it is not necessarily "one" game. The 1992–93 season showed up, and so did a lot of new and untested faces. The season before we had lost seniors Harold Boudreaux, Justin Anderson, T.J. Pugh, and Vernel Singleton. Vernel had been a great four-year player for us, and the other three had all been starters at some point in their careers. We also lost Shaquille, who had taken his game to the NBA. Everybody was counting us out before the first jump ball was tossed.

Bob Gibbons of *All-Star Sports* wrote, "With the departure of franchise Shaquille O'Neal to the pros and virtually all of their frontline, this does not project as a promising year for the Tigers. Coach Dale Brown will truly be a miracle worker if he can go .500 this season." Dick Vitale obviously felt the same when he wrote in his preseason publication, *Dick Vitale Basketball Magazine,* "The Tigers are one of the five teams to attend the last nine NCAA tournaments—they won't make it to ten."

To make a long story short, that team won 20 games, challenged for the division championship, was runner-up in the SEC tournament and made it to our tenth straight NCAA tournament, where we lost to California on a shot at the buzzer by Jason Kidd. Cal went on to upset defending national champion Duke in their next game. After reflecting on the season, I later told my staff that it was a special year where we accomplished things that I am not sure anyone could fully appreciate. One of those accomplishments was the further development of "The Dutchman," Geert Hammink, our 7' post player from the Netherlands.

Geert Hammink is another player who symbolizes what LSU basketball is about. Geert came here from overseas and not only had to learn the LSU basketball system but the American way of life and a new educational system as well. At times he would show flashes of brilliance, yet he could never consistently play at the level we needed to give him the playing time he desired. His freshman year he played in 25 games with no starts and a 2.0 points per game average. After a redshirt year, Geert came back and played in 27 games, starting in only two, and averaging 4.6 points a game. As a junior, he played in 29 games with no starts, and scored 2.4 points a game. As a senior he came into his own.

Life for Geert at LSU as a basketball player was not necessarily easily. He came in at a time where he had to play behind Shaquille O'Neal. He also had to play against Shaq every day in practice, and you've got to believe me when I say that going up against Shaq is not the greatest of things when it comes to building confidence and self-esteem. But Geert had great perseverance. He practiced hard every day and worked hard in each off-season, without any promise of stardom or even a starting position.

When Shaquille went to the pros via hardship, it opened a door for Geert and he pushed it open. As a senior, his numbers went up to 15.3 points a game and he led the Southeastern Conference in rebounding with 10.2 boards a game. He even finished second in the SEC in free throw percentage at .730, which shows even more what a great touch he had for a big man. Geert capped it all off by being drafted in the first round by the Orlando Magic.

Geert practically carried the team on his shoulders in his senior season. He had some great moments, including a 20 point average in three games in Hawaii against Stanford, Duke, and Memphis State, with a 21 point performance against the Blue Devils' Cherokee Parks in Hawaii. He had 21 points and 13 rebounds in a big win for us over Florida; 24 points and 15 rebounds in a home win over Mississippi State; he closed out his home career with 22 points and 18 boards against Ole Miss; and he had two double-doubles against Ole

Miss and Vanderbilt to lead us into the championship game of the SEC tournament.

He is just one of the examples of players at LSU who have overcome numerous hurdles to be successful. To my mind, Geert's greatest accomplishment comes as I am writing this book. Despite the opportunities of professional basketball, Geert is joining Shaquille back on the campus this summer. Geert needed nine hours to graduate and I know that when this book hits the stands, he will have a diploma from LSU.

So there you have just a brief glance at some of the special games, special people, and special efforts that have been a part of LSU basketball since 1972. These games not only shaped and molded the great tradition we have established, but I honestly feel they have gone a long way in building the belief systems of a great number of young men who have put on the LSU uniform. It is for that reason, and not the glory of victory, that I work toward even more special victories.

15

Losing's Lessons

In the building of any championship program, you can always identify several key turning points. During my years at LSU, I can name six: Our first win against Kentucky in 1978; our first SEC championship, which we won in 1979; winning our first SEC tournament in 1980; going to our first Final Four in 1981; proving that wasn't a fluke by doing it again in 1986; and suffering through the 1993–94 season.

I know it may seem odd to include in that list our first losing season in eighteen years. But, having experienced it, I don't believe we could ever win a national championship without learning the lessons we learned during that season.

I always believed that no matter what level of talent we had, I could coach our team to 20 wins and a spot in the NCAA tournament. Imagine how humbling it was to go 11–16 overall and 5–11 in the SEC. Imagine how disappointing it was to have 12 games decided in the last minute, losing 7 of them. Imagine how tough it was to end the season with a 9-game losing streak, the longest streak in my twenty-two years as head coach.

We had it all happen in one year: injuries, overtime losses, a 31-point lead that was wiped away. But I learned more during that season than I ever would have had we pulled out another 20 wins. I believe you should judge a program by how it reacts when it is struggling. I think we reacted with pain, but with class.

Ironically, the turning point in our season didn't occur in November or December. It happened in the summer, months before our first practice. Our point guard Randy Livingston, the national high school player of the year, who I believe would have been among the best guards in all of college basketball, tore up his knee playing basketball at a summer camp where he was working as an instructor. It was questionable whether he would return during the season. He ultimately decided to spend the whole year healing.

Then Andre Owens, who would have been our back-up point guard, became academically ineligible for the first semester. Suddenly, we went from having what I thought was the best point guard combination in the conference to having no point guard at all. The only point guard possibility we had left was a walkon, David Bosley, or converting off-guard Brandon Titus to the point.

The next piece of bad news involved Ronnie Henderson, an All-American high school player at shooting guard who would have teamed up with Randy for one of the best backcourts in the country. Ronnie dislocated his shoulder and needed major surgery. Fortunately, he made a complete recovery and ended up being a real bright star.

Two years earlier we were recruiting what we thought

were the two best high school players in the country, now both of them were hurt.

Then came our problems at center. We had a seven-footer coming in who I promise you would have been a lottery pick in the NBA one day. He was from Europe. Well, while he was attending high school here in the U.S., he wouldn't stand up for our national anthem. He told me he didn't like American foreign policy toward his country. I wasn't sure what to do. But when I was told by his guardian that he had charged $400 calling his friends in Europe, that certainly made the decision easier. We had to ask his guardian to tell him we weren't interested in bringing him to LSU after high school. To make a long story short, he's now playing pro ball in Europe.

So again, we go from having an NBA caliber seven-footer to starting Lenear Burns, a great kid and a hard worker, but a guy who is only 6'6". Our backup was Glover Jackson, who was 6'10", but who weighed only 200 pounds. When you look at the folks we were scheduled to play, Glover was not physically ready for it. We had played five years in a row with a seven-footer of our own. Now our center was 6'6".

All of this is part of the business. You must learn to adjust. I think that's probably as big a part of coaching as recruiting and the strategy of the game.

So we didn't have a point guard, we didn't have a center. Even with that, everything was just so close. We played Arkansas, number one in the country—the national champions— twice to the wire. We played Kentucky and were ahead by 31. They came back and beat us.

We never had a break go our way, but that's sometimes how life is. Everything isn't always roses and championships. But our kids played hard, they stuck together. It's easy to stick together when you're winning—it's a lot harder when you have the kind of year we did.

I think the whole year was summed up by a picture on the front page of the Memphis *Commercial-Appeal* the day after we lost the final game of the year. In the picture, Lenear Burns and Clarence Ceasar were sitting on the bench with their arms around each other. Even in the loss, they were together, they were loving each other.

Yet, other than the game we lost at Auburn, this team never quit playing hard. As a team, they were humiliated. They came into a program that was one of the best in the country, they had a legacy that they had to live up to and didn't do it.

When the season was all over, it woke me up. I realized how far behind we had fallen on the talent scale. I have to admit, I went to sleep at the wheel during our recent recruiting years and I must take full blame for that. I thought we had enough talent. I was obviously wrong.

Having accepted blame for our recruiting mistakes, I want to put an asterisk next to that. Without Emmitt Smith, the Dallas Cowboys were 0–2. The Cowboys weren't going anyplace without him. But once they signed him, they were on their way to winning a second Super Bowl. I truly believe that with Randy, we would have won six or seven more games. He is that valuable to our team. He is our Emmitt Smith.

We will, in the future, have enough talented players to be back on top in college basketball. When I say this year was an important step toward our winning of a national championship, that is why. I learned how much talent we must have and I'm committed to getting that talent to Baton Rouge. If it hadn't been for this year, perhaps I would have had five good players, no bench. We would have gone back to the Final Four and been back in the top ten. But without this lesson, we wouldn't have had the talent to win it all.

The 1993–94 season started out quick with a 20-point win over Texas and an upset of third-ranked Oklahoma State. I hate to admit it, but when we won those two, were 4–0 and ranked in the top twenty-five, I was thinking some pretty vain thoughts. I said to myself, "The touch is still there. I can still get 20 wins even with this team with all the injuries. I didn't know we could be that good." I thought, Boy, I still have the spark.

Instead of being grateful for those wins, I guess I was narcissistic without knowing it. That will never happen again. You need to be humiliated sometimes. And if, as they say, humiliation cleanses the soul, our next game started me on a three-month trip through a damn Spandex washer and dryer facility.

We went to the West Coast for a nationally televised game with UCLA. We were slaughtered. I realized within the first few minutes of the game how big a discrepancy there was in talent. And for the first time, I knew we might be in for a long year. The Bruins, with Shon Tarver and the O'Bannon brothers, were big, quick and talented. I believed that they were a team destined for the Final Four.

I added UCLA, North Carolina, Louisville, Texas, and Oklahoma State to our schedule in an effort to really toughen up this team. Though we were really young, we did have a fairly decent group of veterans. Believing that most of them would be back together the next season, I wanted them to face the best competition I could find, so they wouldn't develop a belief that they were better than they actually were. The year before, we had taken the opposite approach. We had intentionally played an easier schedule so we could pick up wins and gain confidence. The problem with what we were doing was that we had no way of imagining our personnel losses.

During the year, we played nine teams ranked in the top twenty and six from the top ten. We played the defending national champions, North Carolina; the eventual national champions, Arkansas; and some great teams in Kentucky and Louisville. Of all the great teams we played, only two of them—Arkansas and Kentucky—were home games.

In addition to facing great teams, our schedule was filled with great players—and tall players. We played against eleven giant centers during the season—both Eric Montross from North Carolina and Big Country Reeves, who combined to make practically every All-American team, Darnell Robinson and Lee Wilson at Arkansas, Steve Hamer of Tennessee, Andrew DeClerq from Florida, and Charles Claxton at Georgia. We played against more seven-footers during that season than ever before.

All that height, strength, and talent was being guarded by our 6'6" center Lenear Burns. To try and solve that problem, we redesigned our offense to run more and pull the opposing center away from the basket. At times, we ran that offense to perfection. At other times, it looked like we'd never run it in practice.

We paid for it all—no center, no point guard, tough schedule—as the season wore on. The best example of it all falling apart was during our game against Kentucky. We couldn't have asked for a better first half and eventually we led by as many as 31 points. Ronnie Henderson was spectacular. So was Clarence Ceasar. But things started to go downhill in the second half as Kentucky used its depth to wear us down, and fouled our players who started missing free throws. They were mass substituting, something we just couldn't do.

Then Clarence and Lenear each picked up a fourth foul. I took them both out of the game and within three minutes, Kentucky cut 10 points off the lead. I had to put them both back in and Clarence quickly fouled out. Still, we could have won if we just made our free throws down the stretch. We didn't.

Losing's Lessons

The same free-throw shooting problem killed us in the Arkansas game at home. We were ahead 92–90 with ten seconds to go. Andre Owens was fouled and had two free throws coming. We called time out to try and take the pressure off, reminding him that no matter what happened, we were still ahead. We told the rest of the team to run a contained press after the second free throw. I told our players to foul any Arkansas player because we had a foul to waste. Andre hit only one free throw. Arkansas passed the ball up quickly and none of our guys fouled like we had planned. Instead, we went for a steal and didn't get it. Arkansas hit a three-pointer from outer space to send it into overtime, and they beat us.

Then to top it all, we went to the SEC tournament in Memphis to play Georgia. We had finished the regular season by losing seven straight, including those heartbreakers to Kentucky and Arkansas. We fell behind early to Georgia. Partly through the first half, I got two technical fouls and—for only the second time in my forty years of coaching—was sent to the locker room.

What followed was one of the most challenging moments of my career. Everything inside of me told me to openly take on the system, to explain why I felt the referees were wrong. But my daughter challenged me with a little book called *Our Daily Bread*. An entry in that book encouraged me to speak with a prudent tongue. I decided to do something I can't remember ever doing before, and that was to be silent. I decided not to become the story.

We lost the game and there was a locker room full of players who had played hard, and whom I felt I had let down. As I watched our guys sitting there crying, I realized that these were guys who had just completed a losing season. Yet it hurt as much as losing a game for the national championship.

The day after we lost in the SEC tournament, I started to

work immediately on the recruiting problem. I flew from Memphis to Kentucky to recruit the runner-up for Mr. Basketball in Kentucky, Tony Pietrowski, an outstanding guard. We have three redshirts who will join next year's team, guard Randy Livingston and centers Misha Mutavdjic and Alonzo Johnson, both 6'11". We signed a former high school All-American named Landers Nolley, who had gone to Hiawassee Junior College in Tennessee. At 6'8", he can play several positions for us. We signed Garrick Scott, a 6'9" forward from Panola Junior College. We also signed Adam Walton, who at 6'9" will eventually be a really good player for us. He just has to get over the pressure that must come with being the son of Hall of Fame center Bill Walton. Finally, we signed Jolay Palfi, a 6'9" perimeter player from Yugoslavia.

So there will be eight new faces on the floor for us next year. Quite a change. The most noticeable difference will be in size. We will have nine guys on the team taller than the 6'6" center we started in 1993–94. Fitting that many new players into our system will present its own set of challenges. It will take a little while to get off the ground, but I'm really looking forward to it.

The only downside off the court for this team came in the classroom. In February, we had a team meeting on the subject. To start the meeting out, I had Roman Roubtchenko stand up. I told the team that this young man, who came to America just 2½ years ago, had our team's highest grade point average. Then I called on six other players and had them stand. "You six have three things in common, in addition to having the lowest grade point averages on our team," I said. "Each of you are native Americans, you're basketball players and you're black. When are we going to end the cycle of this constant lack of education and enthusiasm for education among black athletes in our country?"

I then wrote the number 34 on the blackboard. I asked them if any of them knew the significance of the number. Only Alonzo Johnson, who grew up in Selma, Alabama, knew what it meant, and he knew because I had shared the story with him when I was recruiting him. The story is about southern slaves who would sneak books out of their masters' homes to try and teach themselves how to read. When they were caught, they were given 34 lashes for trying to educate themselves. Still, they didn't stop sneaking books out. By the way, Alonzo will wear the jersey number 34 when he plays for LSU.

"What amazes me," I told the team, "is that we damn near have to lash some of you to get you to go to class. And in five years, when *USA Today* comes by to do their story about graduation rates, you won't be the ones to be embarrassed by the numbers. I will be blamed. This university will be blamed. But they won't blame you."

So this experience also helped me redefine my goals for the future. It is a big change on my part. I have always been for the underdog and minority in my life. If it was women who weren't being equally paid or a Hispanic group, a Jewish group, or a black group, they've always had my support.

But I'm now changing my philosophy. I'm really going to be for the underdog. And my new definition of an underdog and minority will have no color, no religion, no sex, and no ethnic background. That minority is someone who wants to work for everything they get in life, to do it honorably, to make the world a better place, to live in, and to get educated.

I'm not going to be any different from Nelson Mandela. In an interview right before the South African elections, he said, "Twenty-seven years I spent in prison for a philosophy I have, the philosophy that all men should be treated equal and all men should be free. However, the black man of South Africa must know that in order to have those things, he must be educated, disciplined, and persevering." That, too, is going to be my standard. That is the greatest underdog in the world.

I'm sick of guys not wanting to be educated. It takes the fun out of the job. Education sets you free.

I am sure that in addition to winning and losing and the importance of schoolwork, our guys learned many lessons during the year. I did, too. I learned just how much we as a society focus on winning, on possessing things like Gucci purses, Rolex watches, fancy cars, and gold medals.

Well, all those folks who judge only on winning are wrong. This team was a champion. This team did just as John Wooden's father told John to do when he said, "Johnny, this is a very competitive world. Whatever you do, never try to be better than anyone else. But never cease to be the best that you can be." For the most part, we did the best we could do.

But doing your best doesn't matter anymore. We forget who won the silver because the only person who gets all the attention is the one with the gold. The Nancy Kerrigan–Tonya Harding story is a great example. Was winning really so important that Tonya Harding was willing to have someone hurt?

But Kerrigan didn't show much humility. She went to the Olympics and won the silver medal, finishing behind the girl from Ukraine. This girl was a fifteen-year-old orphan who had lost her mother and father. She grew up with nothing. Yet Kerrigan complained that she should have won the gold. She could have—should have—shown class by congratulating the other girl and saying how great it was that she had the opportunity to compete and represent her country. She could have said how great it was to enjoy this bright spot in her otherwise difficult life.

As I sat and thought about all this, I realized I have been guilty of this same mindset in the past. On the wall of my office in the Pete Maravich Assembly Center, I hung pictures of all of my winning teams—teams that have been to the Final Four, SEC champion teams, Top Ten teams. That was wrong. I went back after the season and added a picture of the 1993–94 team because they were champions too.

If there was a Jonathan Livingston Seagull in the coaching profession, I was it. I was the free spirit. But I wasn't truly free until I lost. Losing also helped me realize how much I do love these kids. It proved to me I didn't just love these guys because they were winning for us, or because we were always competing for top national honors. But here was a group of kids I loved as much as any group I've ever coached. They didn't have a lot of talent. They weren't very big. They didn't pay attention to detail. But they were nice people. They tried their best. I'll always remember them as champions.

My wise friend John Wooden has always said, "When you are through learning, you are through," and this past year was an education. I am amazed that the longer I coach and live, the more Coach Wooden's words gain in strength. I never thought that complacency would make its way into my daily life, but it did. Years of success only seemed to fertilize it.

The word "complacency" itself is a word that we hear a great deal. Coaches use it when talking to their teams. We warn them about this ugly monster, as we do not want it to creep up from behind us and trip us, making us short of our goals. It is a word that I have heard or used ever since I have been involved with athletics, but not until this year did I really know what that word meant or the lessons it would teach. One lesson is that talking about it does not ward it off; it won't shield you from this terrible disease.

The second lesson is that it can happen to anybody. I certainly never thought it could happen to me, because as much as I enjoy winning, I absolutely hate losing. Sure, I had read about it. In *Season on the Brink*, Coach Knight talked about how he got complacent in recruiting for a couple of years and it caught up to Indiana. Coach Knight? Complacent? It can happen to anyone—including me!

Above all, I learned the true definition of complacency. You see, all these years that I had heard and used this word, I really had no idea what it meant. I had been under the impression that complacency was when you let up slightly or let your guard down. But nothing could be further from the truth. Our staff worked just as hard this year as they had the past couple of years. Our players had worked about as hard. I felt that my work ethic was on course with past seasons. What we forgot, however, was the fact that this great game of basketball is a game of levels and played by fierce competitors.

Letting up is not complacency. It is being able to take it to the next level. You see, we as individuals and together as a team have to find ways to dig down deeper and find a way to work even harder. Often we say, "How can we work harder?" Trust me, we can.

Because of all that we have accomplished through the years, with our grand tradition and reputation, we must increase our effort and dedication. That starts with me. One thing that tradition does is put a target on your chest. It motivates your opponents to play against you at levels that they cannot play at in other games. This is extremely difficult for players to understand, but it is critical to know. An example was this past season when we traveled to Oxford to play the University of Mississippi. Ole Miss had a winning record; we were limping in with a losing record, along with seven consecutive defeats. Still, Ole Miss had one of the largest crowds of the year and their players played with an emotion that we had not seen in previous Rebel game films. It was the game of the year for them, and they blitzed us. After winning the game, their players were ecstatic. Many fans ran onto the floor.

There was one other final lesson that I learned from complacency. It is often like a cancer that grows throughout the entire body and is discovered at a late stage. It cannot be quickly corrected. We started the season with upset wins over no. 24 Texas and no. 3 Oklahoma State. In our first three SEC road games, we lost at no. 1 Arkansas by one point, to Final Four participant Florida by one point, and upset no. 19 Vanderbilt, their first regular season loss at home in three years.

But the cancer was already in there. I realized it early, and actually sounded out a warning to our staff and players. We had let up some on recruiting. We let up slightly in discipline. We tried to correct things during the season, but the disease had gone too deep in us. The only medicine is major surgery in the offseason. We will be back, but there are no midseason cures.

Still, it was complacency that taught me even more about what I need to achieve to reach our goals and continue our journey. Life, after all, is a journey, not a destination. I am more prepared and more excited about that trip than ever before.

16

Last of the Dinosaurs

For years, as I was coming up through the coaching profession, I heard successful coaches say that it was easier getting to the top than staying there. I always thought that was just a cliché, a way for the top guys to try to make others feel sorry for them. I was wrong. It *is* tough to stay there.

There are only nine coaches who have been at the same Division I school for more than twenty-two years: Dean Smith, Bobby Knight, Don Haskins, Peter Carril, Norm Stewart, Pete Cassidy, Jim Phelan, Denny Crum, and me. Those others on the list led Pat O'Brien, one of the best sportscasters in the business, to call us "the last of the dinosaurs."

Think of how much money you could have won if in 1972 you would have bet that twenty-three years later, Dale Brown would still be the coach at LSU.

There are an awful lot of reasons why you can't stay at one

school or stay on top of the profession for very long anymore.

The first reason is that you get spoiled by success. When you win, winning no longer becomes good enough. Now you've got to win it all. The fans get spoiled. The media gets spoiled. And the truth is, you spoil yourself, too. And that level of expected excellence is never lowered. To stay on top, you have to learn to accept high expectations. You have to be careful that you don't become a victim of them, that you don't become tense believing you have to win every game. The second that happens, you're on the road to self-destruction. You no longer enjoy what you've accomplished. You also have to be careful of success, as I told Shaquille once, and not allow it to steal your own freedom, your time, and your personality.

Sometimes you build your own monster, so to speak, and that's why there are some that don't last. I don't think you can last if you're in it for the cheers or you worry about the jeers because there is always gonna be a down time. We beat Tulane University sixteen straight times. A number of years ago, we played them in the NIT tournament and we lost. You would have thought our program had fallen apart. The headline the next morning read: TULANE UNIVERSITY WHIPS THE TIGERS. Isn't it funny how soon they forget.

Another key to longevity in this business is credibility. Anybody can be a flash in the pan. Anybody can come in to a program and have a new motto, a new slogan or saying. But it doesn't take long for the people of a community to see through all that if you're only in it for yourself. There are a lot of coaches who think they should move every five years because they believe you use up your coupons, so to speak, in a community. But I think if you're honest and not a fake, they'll give you more coupons. That's certainly been my experience in Baton Rouge.

You also have to understand the politics of your environment. I've watched over the years as a lot of people in this state were lined up in the sniper's scope and eventually shot out of the saddle for one thing or another—from governors to evangelists to coaches to athletic directors. They were politically assassinated because this is a tough state to survive in. In Louisiana, you can go back and look at the record books, there aren't many things that can exist for twenty-three years.

The only way I've survived here is by being smart enough to keep my ear to the rail. I know when the engine starts, I know how many cars it's pulling, I know how far it's going and I know how fast it's going. In my time, LSU has had four athletic directors. It's had six football coaches. I've seen forty-three coaches in the SEC come and go. I've seen fifty-eight coaches from schools in the state of Louisiana.

Another key to staying at the top is surrounding yourself with assistants who make up for your weaknesses. Bear Bryant, whom I was fortunate enough to get to know while he was at Alabama, once told me that that was the key to his success. He said putting together a winning program was easy, "as long as you remember there's no one guy that knows everything about everything."

I've tried to live by that rule ever since. I don't think staffs get enough credit. If you go to practices run by top coaches who are confident and successful, you'd be shocked at how their staffs work. Go to Duke's practice sometime, or one of ours at LSU, and you'll see this principle at work.

Lefty Driesell said once that when he hired somebody, he didn't want them to be a tactician or recruiter. He wanted them to be a close friend who would tell him the truth. That's good advice, too. You must have an inner circle of love. That circle of love must say it exactly like it is. They have to come to meetings when I've got some wild idea and say, "We can't do that, Dale, we don't have the talent or the depth or the experience." But after the debate, we all have to walk out and then defend and love each other and enjoy each other. There has to be total support.

Just remember this: twenty-one of the most notable civilizations that have ever been founded crumbled from within and not without (Norman Vincent Peale). A great number of coaches who get fired had some assistant coach out there fanning the fire. The assistant was either bad-mouthing the coach to an administrator or the press—always off the record, of course. When the players know you love each other, they can see it and it's almost contagious. But when the players know that there's friction, they can seize upon it.

Some insecure coaches try to hire "yes men," but I don't think you can grow that way. Look at the guys who assisted John Wooden at UCLA and you'll see what I mean.

I've been blessed over the years to have a long string of talented and loyal assistant coaches who have made up for my weaknesses.

Another support system, your family, must exist for a coach to stay at the top of this business. With my wife Vonnie, my daughter Robyn, son-in-law Chris, and grandson Christopher, I've had the love and the peace to put up with all that comes with being a head coach.

My wife of thirty-five years has not been one to whine and mope about the hours this job takes. She really lets me be me. I don't like to be fenced in and restricted. She's provided that liberty for me. When I come home, I don't come home to arguments. I don't come home to tension. I've watched a lot of others be destroyed by those things.

When times have been tough, she's left me little notes that make all the difference in the world. Imagine the patience it must have taken to live with someone as aggressive as me. I'm not sure there is another woman who could have lived with me. As I get older, and I see a few lines in Vonnie's face, I think to myself I've really been blessed to have her in my life. I probably appreciate Vonnie more now than I ever have before.

Robyn has been a son and a daughter and a buddy all in one. She has so fulfilled everything for me through her love that I never felt any void in not having a son. She's bright, gentle but strong, and, like her mother, very honest with me. I can talk to her about anything. I never wanted to turn her into an athlete, though she could have been a good athlete. She's maintained her own identity. I think many times the wives and family of coaches join in the hero worshiping. They become cheerleaders. That's not true of Vonnie and Robyn.

I've said many times that I can whip the world as long as I continue to have those two circles in my life—my family at home and my basketball family.

In my forty years of coaching, the game has certainly progressed—or in some cases, retrogressed. You now have to teach the fundamentals more than you ever had to before. Ironically, as the talent level of the players has risen, the level of fundamentals has disappeared. Basketball has become a television extravaganza—just throw the ball up and as you dunk it, firecrackers go off all over the arena. I do think the reasons are television, the NBA, and the number of well-publicized slam dunk contests that exist.

These kids have all this talent, but they don't understand the most elementary things like how to lead a player when you are passing the ball. Passing has become almost a lost art, as have dribbling and reading defenses. I was not nearly the athlete that the guys I'm coaching are, but I always had a knowledge of the game.

I began to notice this phenomenon when Jack Schalow and I came here in our first year and we could not get the players to run a zone offense. The two of us went out there and had to demonstrate it in a two-on-two game against a couple of our players. I ran the baseline and had Jack play the high post. The two of us, two North Dakotans, cut those players to pieces. Well, we were drilled since the fifth grade on our fundamentals, while a lot of these kids were so good it seemed they were left alone by their high school coaches. I've had high school coaches tell me that too much teaching was like putting a bit in the mouth of those athletes. I disagree. I think it does those young players a disservice if you don't teach them.

Larry Bird existed because of his fundamentals. I didn't think Magic Johnson had great talent. I think Magic was very much like Larry Bird. But Magic was the Leonardo da Vinci of the basketball court because he used his mind. Magic couldn't run, Magic couldn't jump, Magic wasn't very quick. Magic couldn't shoot for years. But Magic could analyze. He had the game down and had great fundamentals.

We had one player who, when he went to catch the ball, he had his thumbs in the wrong position. That sounds simple, almost silly. But it is part of the fundamentals. Now some guys, when you tell them that, their reaction is, "Coach, I can run the floor and dunk. Why are you worried about my thumbs?"

The other major change that's occurred over the years in college sports is the responsibility of the coach. It used to be that we had to win to keep our jobs. Then, because of Title IX and all the gender equity requirements, basketball and football coaches had to make a lot of money for their schools to fund the non-revenue sports. Now we are responsible for the graduation of every athlete. When are we going to start making our athletes accountable? When do the parents step up and get involved? Why is everything the responsibility of the university or the coach? I never once felt my college coach had anything to do with my academic background.

Before I get out of coaching, I'm sure they'll add a fourth dimension: every athlete has to be canonized as a saint before he leaves your team. It has become ridiculous.

Once I do get out of coaching, I know now what my plans are. Given all that I've been fortunate enough to do and accomplish, I was worried about what could keep me interested and excited. I've done a lot of traveling, so that won't do it. I'm not interested in doing television color commentary. Then recently I saw a commercial for a group that helps the poor and the needy overseas. That was it. People all over the world are starving, uneducated, in need of clothes and schools. I decided that I could really make a difference for those people. I know a lot of wealthy people who could help. I want to put together my own independent organization to make a difference.

One of the most interesting perspectives about success that's been shared with me came from country music star Kenny Rogers. I interviewed Kenny once for our *LSU Basketball* television show. I said, "It's funny that in athletics, many people look at the teams on top and just assume they've always been there. Now you have the number one song in the country. Do you meet people who think the same?" He answered, "It's funny, but for twenty-two years I worked and never had a song in the top fifty. When I finally became successful, I realized how glad I was for those twenty-two years. You have to enjoy the climb because too many people, once they get there, don't get to stay long. It is like mountain climbing. The folks that scale Mount Everest or Mount McKinley, they don't stay there very long. They get up there and come back down. So if you don't enjoy the beauty and the climb and rocks and the dangers, there's no sense in climbing. I decided I was going to enjoy my climb."

Like Kenny Rogers, I'm enjoying the climb. I know we are going to win a national championship someday. I know Norman Vincent Peale's prediction will be right. But while I've never been more confident of it, I've also never been less consumed by it. I'm not going to work toward that championship. I'm just going to work knowing that we *will* win it. And I'm going to enjoy the work and count all my many blessings.